# THE SMALL BUSINESS INFORMATION SOURCE BOOK

a/w

# THE SMALL BUSINESS INFORMATION SOURCE BOOK

## ADRIAN A. PARADIS

**BETTERWAY PUBLICATIONS, INC.**
WHITE HALL, VIRGINIA

Published by Betterway Publications, Inc.
Box 81
White Hall, VA 22987

Cover design by Deborah B. Chappell
Typography by Superior Type

**Library of Congress Cataloging-in-Publication Data**

Paradis, Adrian A.
    The small and home business information source book.

    Includes index.
    1. Small business — Information services — United States.
2. Home-based businesses — Information services — United
States. I. Title.
HD2346.U5P37      1987            658′.022′07073          87-15925
ISBN 0-932620-81-7 (pbk.)

Printed in the United States of America
0  9  8  7  6  5  4  3  2  1

# Contents

## A WORD TO THE READER

Please read this brief foreword before you look through the book. It will enable you to use it to the best advantage and avoid missing the information you may be seeking.

The comprehensive index is the key to unlocking all the information in Part I which includes almost 150 principal subjects. Therefore, whenever you use this book, first go to the index. The topic or data you are seeking may appear in Part I under a different name, but the numerous cross-indexes should enable you to locate it quickly.

The book is arranged in two sections: Part I: *Subjects,* and Part II: *Organizations.* The second part contains an alphabetical listing of associations, government agencies, and societies which are not included in Part I. If you cannot find a particular organization in Part II, it may be mentioned in Part I and you will need to locate it through the index.

The appendices contain a simplified glossary of the more common business and financial terms. Full names and addresses of all publishers mentioned in Part I also will be found in the appendices under: "Publishers' Addresses."

Mention of a particular organization or service offered by a group is not an endorsement of that group or any service. The reference merely indicates what is available and the reader must determine independently whether or not it is suitable for his or her needs.

## A WORD TO THE READER (continued)

Every effort has been made to ensure accuracy of names, telephone numbers, and addresses. However, ours is a mobile society and undoubtedly some of these addresses and phone numbers will change even as the book rolls off the press.

The editor wishes to thank the many organizations which so generously provided information and data. He is also grateful for the unlimited use of the Littleton Public Library and the extensive libraries of Dartmouth College. The help and patience of the Directory Assistance telephone personnel in each of the fifty states should also be acknowledged.

Finally, should any reader find it impossible to locate the source of sorely needed information, the editor will be glad to try his hand at no charge if a letter is addressed to him care of the publisher.

Adrian A. Paradis

Sugar Hill
New Hampshire
June 15, 1987

# Part I
# Subjects

# ABSENTEEISM

No matter whether it is giant General Motors or a small business with three employees, absenteeism can be a serious problem. Back in the days of the garment sweat shops, one Manhattan employer put up a sign announcing: "If you don't come in Sunday, don't come in Monday." Fortunately this ruthless labor practice is a thing of the past but the pendulum has swung over to the opposite extreme.

Today, if an employee does not feel like going to work or has a good reason for staying away, he or she may rationalize the absenteeism in accordance with the current thinking that the individual should come first, that it is perfectly all right to twist the truth if necessary, or that a missed day makes no difference. The conscientious employee is the exception in many work places and, like it or not, the average employer is forced to deal with this current attitude toward work and responsibility.

While it is perfectly legal and correct to penalize absenteeism by witholding pay for a day not worked, provided warning has been given either in published employee regulations or in a memorandum to the offending individual, this does not solve the problem. Since it is often impractical to appeal to an employee's sense of loyalty and/or honesty, it may prove better to offer rewards for perfect attendance. Many companies give an extra day of paid vacation for a certain number of days worked without an absence, or they offer other inducements.

Some of the books listed below should help you resolve the problem. If you belong to a trade association, a chamber of commerce, or other business group, possibly you can attend seminars on the subject or obtain helpful advice from members faced with the same problem.

## Suggested References

Chadwich-Jones, J.K. and Colin Brown, *Social Psychology of Absenteeism*. New York, Praeger Publishers, 1982.

Jones, Dallas L. et al, editors, *Reducing Worker Absenteeism*. Ann Arbor, Mich., Industrial Development Division of Institute of Science and Technology.

Kovach, Kenneth, *Organization Size, Job Satisfaction, Absenteeism and Turnover*. Lanham, Md., University Press of America, 1977.

# ACADEMIC CREDENTIALS

According to a 1985 congressional investigation some 500,000 Americans hold fraudulant degrees from diploma-mill schools. Many customers of these institutions know what they are buying, but some do not. The point is that you could hire an unqualified applicant with false credentials. Even a diploma appearing to be from an accredited institution could be suspect. One Oregon company sold some 2,000 fake diplomas, purporting to be from some 300 legitimate universities in the United States, Canada and England.

Checking accreditation is your best guarantee that a college or university has met a number of rigid standards and requirements set by an accrediting board. Therefore, unless you recognize the name of the college or university which an applicant asserts is his alma mater, it is advisable to check (to see if it is accredited) by referring to the college directories. If the school is not listed, contact the state department of education to check on the school's accreditation.

Should you have reason to suspect that an applicant is not actually a graduate of the school for which he produces a diploma, ask the alumnae office to verify that he is a graduate.

## Suggested References

*Barron's Guide to the Two Year Colleges*. Woodbury, NY, Barron's Educational Services, Inc., annual.

*Lovejoys College Guide*. New York, Monarch Press, annual.

*Peterson's Four Year Colleges*. Princeton, NJ, Peterson's Guides, annual.

**Note:** One or more of the above should be in your public library or the high school guidance department library.

# ACCOUNTING

*Accounting* is defined here as a system of classifying, analyzing and summarizing business and financial records to show the operation in terms of profit and loss. In contrast, the term *bookkeeping* is the process of recording systematically the accounts or transactions of money. Since each industry has developed its own accounting methods, there is a wide range of literature on the subject just as there are several specialized accounting institutes or societies listed in Gale's *Encyclopedia of Associations.*

One organization which may be of interest is the National Association of Accountants founded in 1919. As is the case with many professional organizations, it stresses its professional services, the most important of which is its Certified Management Accountant Program. Over 6,000 certificates have been awarded up to the mid-1980s and it was expected that the number would double within two years' time. The Controllers Council and the Business Planning Board are two other valuable activities, plus the wide range of publications available to members and non-members, on almost every aspect of business finance and financial planning.

## For Further Information:

National Association of Accountants
10 Paragon Drive
Montvale, NJ 07645
Phone: 201-573-9000

## Suggested References

Doyle, Dennis M., *Efficient Accounting and Record Keeping.* (Wiley Small Business Series). New York, John Wiley & Sons, 1977.

Midgett, Elwin W., *Accounting Primer.* New York, New American Library, 1971.

Perry, William E., *What To Ask Your Accountant: A Reference for Those in Business and Those About to Begin.* New York, Beaufort Books, 1982.

**Note:** Consult the subject volume of *Books in Print* for the titles of accounting books which may be of special help or interest to you.

# ADVERTISING

Advertising is big business but large corporations which advertise on the radio and TV or in newspapers and periodicals do not have an exclusive grip on professional advertising services. In many communities individuals and small agencies offer services within the reach of the small or medium size business. Some business owners are able to plan, write, and place their advertising themselves. If you feel capable of doing this, some of the books listed below may prove helpful. On the other hand, should this not be your forte, consult the yellow pages under "Advertising Agencies and Consultants" and you may be surprised at what working with a professional can accomplish within a reasonable budget.

## Suggested References

Amstell, I. Joel, *What You Should Know About Advertising.* Dobbs Ferry, NY, Business Almanac Series No. 17, Oceana, 1969.

Bellavance, Diane, *Advertising and Public Relations for a Small Business.* Boston, DBA Books, 1985.

Cook, Harvey, *Profitable Advertising Techniques for Small Businesses.* Reston, VA, Reston Publishing, 1981.

Council of Better Business Bureaus, Inc., *Do's and Don'ts in Advertising Copy.* Arlington, VA, Council of Better Business Bureaus, Inc., loose leaf, updated monthly.

Gray, Ernest A., *Profitable Methods for Small Business Advertising.* New York, Wiley Series on Small Business Management, 1–471, John Wiley & Sons, 1984.

Hollingworth, Harry L., *Advertising and Selling: Principles of Appeal and Response.* New York, Garland Publishing, 1985.

Milton, Shirley F., *Advertising for Modern Retailers.* New York, Fairchild Books and Visuals, 1974.

Siegel, G. M., *How to Advertise and Promote Your Business.* El Segundo, CA, TC Publications, 1978.

**See also:** DIRECT MAIL

# AFFIRMATIVE ACTION

In 1965 President Lyndon Johnson first used the term "affirmative action" when he ordered contractors to take affirmative action in hiring minorities, asserting that equal employment opportunity is a right to be enjoyed without regard to national origin, race, religion or sex. This had already been mandated by the Civil Rights Act of 1964 and later by the Equal Employment Opportunity Act of 1972. Violators should be reported to the Equal Employment Opportunity Commission which may bring cases to court if necessary.

Affirmative action programs identify jobs closed to minorities and women, describe steps that employers must take to correct deficiencies in employment practices, set goals and times for actually achieving such affirmative action, and attempt to recruit minorities and women and train them. Large companies with government contracts must have affirmative action programs. Many state and local governments also require affirmative action plans.

Your state labor department can tell you whether the legislature has passed affirmative action laws and if so, whether you are covered by the legislation. For information on the federal level, see below.

## For Further Information

Equal Employment Opportunity Commission
Office of Program Operations
2401 E Street, NW
Washington, DC 20507
Phone 202-634-6922
Requests for general information may be made also over a nationwide toll-free telephone number: 800-USA–EEOC.

# ALCOHOLISM

Alcoholism among employees is a widespread and seldom admitted problem for large and small businesses. One of the most effective means of dealing with it is to refer addicted individuals to the nearest Alcoholics Anonymous group or alcoholism treatment center. Families of alcoholics may find encouragement, help, and support from the local Al Anon.

## For Further Information

National Council on Alcoholism
12 West 21 Street
New York, NY 10010
Phone: 212-206-6770
Publishes books, pamphlets, and catalogs on aspects of alcoholism and its treatment; maintains 2,000+ volume library; works to control and prevent alcoholism.

Al-Anon Family Group Headquarters
One Park Avenue
New York, NY 10016
Phone: 212-683-1771
This is the headquarters office for the international organization established to help relatives and friends of those afflicted with alcoholism. Alateen welcomes young people 12–20 years of age whose lives have suffered because of someone else's alcoholism, often a parent. For the nearest group consult your local telephone directory or contact the headquarters office.

Alcoholics Anonymous World Services
PO Box 459
Grand Central Station
New York, NY 10163
Phone: 212-686-1100
This organization popularly known as "AA" needs no introduction nor description except to mention that a million individuals belong to some 35,000 groups scattered about the country. These are men and women who find strength and help through meeting together regularly with others who have the same affliction and sharing their experiences and fellowship. Thus they try to solve both their own and others' problems. For the nearest Alcoholics Anonymous group consult your local telephone directory or contact the headquarters office.

To learn the location of treatment centers and points where you may obtain information about

## ALCOHOLISM (continued)

alcoholism, look in the yellow pages of the phone book under "Alcoholism Information and Treatment Centers." There are a number of specialized groups which help alcoholics and which are listed in Gale's *Encyclopedia of Associations.*

## AMERICAN DATES AND FACTS

*The Encyclopedia of American Facts and Dates* contains over 15,000 facts, dates, and events in American history beginning in the year 986 and ending in 1986. It is arranged by date and subject. For any given year—and often by specific months and days—it presents information in four categories placed side by side: (1) Exploration and Settlement; Wars; Government; Civil rights; Statistics; (2) Publishing; Arts and Music; Popular Entertainment; Architecture; Theater; (3) Business and Industry; Science; Education; Philosophy and Religion; and (4) Sports; Social Issues and Crime; Folkways; Fashion; Holidays.

**Suggested References**

*The Encyclopedia of American Facts and Dates.* Cincinnati, Writer's Digest, 1987.

# ANNUAL REPORTS

Preparation of the corporate annual report is usually the responsibility of the corporate secretary and/or the financial officer. To obtain sample copies of other corporate reports write to the Office of the Secretary of each company for which a report is desired. See CORPORATE INFORMATION for the company names, addresses, and listings of principal officers.

**Suggested References**

Anderson, Anker, *Graphing Financial Information.* Montvale, NJ, National Association of Accountants.

Opinion Research Corporation, *Telling the Company's Financial Story.* Morristown, NJ, Financial Executives Research Foundation, 1964.

Solomon, Morton B., et. al., *Main Hurdmen Guide to Preparing Financial Reports.* New York, John Wiley & Sons, 1984.

Williams, Patrick, *The Employee Annual Report: Purpose, Format and Content.* Chicago, Lawrence Ragan Communications, 1983.

# ANTITRUST

The Clayton Antitrust Act of 1914 outlawed price discrimination that favored one buyer over another. It forbid anticompetitive agreements in which a seller would sell only to dealers who agreed not to handle the products or services of another business. Other laws prohibited price-fixing agreements among companies which were designed to fix the price of a service or product or to do this and maintain a monopoly.

The Assistant Attorney General (United States) is in charge of the Antitrust Division of the Department of Justice and is responsible for enforcing federal antitrust laws. These laws "affect virtually all industries and apply to every phase of business, including manufacturing, transportation, distribution and marketing. They prohibit a variety of practices that restrain trade, such as price-fixing conspiracies, corporate mergers likely to reduce the competitive vigor of particular markets, and predatory acts designed to achieve or maintain monopoly power."

**Suggested References**

Garrett, James, *Antitrust Compliance:* A Legal and Business Guide. New York, Practicing Law Institute, 1978.

Kinter, Earl W., *Anti-Trust Primer.* New York, Macmillan, 1973.

Matto, Edward A., *A Manager's Guide to the Antitrust Laws.* New York, AMACOM, 1980.

Van Cise, Jerrold and William T. Lifland, *Understanding the Antitrust Laws.* New York, Practicing Law Institute, 1980.

# ARBITRATION

Arbitration is an important element in solving labor disputes. In addition, many commercial contracts contain a clause making arbitration mandatory in the event of a disagreement over the terms or execution of the agreement. The American Arbitration Association encourages and develops the use of arbitration in labor and commercial relations as well as international trade. It offers the services of innumerable skilled arbitrators who operate under established procedural rules and help settle commercial, labor, accident and international disputes.

According to the American Arbitration Association "the most frequently arbitrated disputes concern discipline, discharge, demotion, staffing, promotion, productivity, pensions, seniority and safety. Streamlined procedures for the settlement of labor-management disputes have been formulated. Under expedited procedures, disputes can be heard quickly, and the decision of the arbitrator must be handed down within several days after the close of the hearing. When employees are not members of a union, it is possible for their employer to submit grievances to an impartial arbitrator. This can be provided for in the personnel manual or can be arranged on a case-by-case basis.

"AAA's publications are designed to keep labor-management professionals and others who serve the labor community well informed of policies and procedures in dispute settlement. Through these publications, the knowledge of experienced professionals is made available to all."

## For Further Information

American Arbitration Association
140 West 51 Street
New York, NY 10020
Phone: 212-484-4000

## Suggested References

Coulson, Robert, *Business Arbitration: What You Need to Know.* New York, American Arbitration Association, 1982.

Daniels, Gene and Kenneth Gagala, *Labor Guide to Negotiating Wages and Benefits.* Englewood Cliffs, NJ, Reston Publishing, 1985.

# ARBITRATION (continued)

Nolan, Dennis R., *Labor Arbitration Law and Practice in a Nutshell.* St. Paul, MN, West Publishing, 1979.

Palmer, John R., *The Use of Accounting Information in Labor Negotiations.* Montvale, NJ, National Association of Accountants.

In addition to the above you will want to consider many of the fine books published by the American Arbitration Association. Send for their "AAA Catalog of Publications for Business People and Those Who Represent Them."

## ASSOCIATIONS

The standard reference work for locating the names of associations and societies is Gale's *Encyclopedia of Associations.* The third volume is a comprehensive index which enables the user to find an association listing by name or subject. Both the *World Almanac* and the *Information Please Almanac* contain short listings of associations and societies.

A selected list of associations, government agencies and societies not mentioned in Part I of this book, but of interest to many business owners and managers, will be found in Part II.

### Directories

Colgate, Craig, Jr. and John Russell, eds., *National Trade and Professional Associations of the United States.* Washington, DC, Columbia Books, 1985.

Gruber, Katherine, ed., *Encyclopedia of Associations.* Detroit, Gale, annual.

## BETTER BUSINESS BUREAUS

The first Better Business Bureau was established in 1914 as a movement to enable business leaders to set standards for national advertising as well as eliminate selling abuses. Today Better Business Bureaus help protect both the public and business from questionable business practices, false representation, dishonest or abusive business practices, and fraud. Further information about the organizations as well as how to start a local bureau may be obtained from the national council.

### For Further Information

Council of Better Business Bureaus
1515 Wilson Boulevard
Arlington, VA 22209
Phone: 703-276-0100

Mention should also be made of the numerous Better Business Bureau booklets on wise buying, tip sheets on consumer information, philanthropy, arbitration, business advisory subjects, etc. The subjects are too numerous to list here but many of these inexpensive booklets will be of interest to most businessmen. Write to the council at the above address and ask for "Booklets on Wise Buying."

## BIOGRAPHICAL INFORMATION

Obtaining biographical information about living people is not easy but by no means impossible either. Some suggested sources follow.

The most sensible way to undertake a search is to tell the reference librarian at your public or nearest college library the name, occupation, and approximate birth date of the individual you want to investigate. Difficult searches call for the expertise of a trained librarian, however, in the event there is no reference librarian available, you can do your own search.

The Marquis Company which publishes the well-known *Who's Who in America* publishes over a dozen other biographical directories. In addition, numerous other Who's Who and various biographical directories covering a wide range of professions and businesses can be found in larger libraries, and may be available in yours.

After consulting the Who's Who directories available to you, search the following: the library catalog; the author volumes of *Books in Print*; the *Biography Index*; the *New York Times Index*; the *Reader's Guide to Periodical Literature*; other pertinent indexes in the library.

If unsuccessful, call the state library at the state capitol. Someone there may be able to help or suggest other reference sources.

## BLUE CROSS–BLUE SHIELD GROUP RATES

No matter how small your company may be, you are probably eligible to join a group which offers Blue Cross-Blue Shield insurance. This national insurance underwriter of medical insurance encourages such membership because it reduces its administrative costs and enables it to pass along some savings to the group. In some parts of the country several associations offer the coverage to businesses. One such group is the Independent Retail Business Association based in Waterbury, Vermont, which serves a five-state area.

For the names and addresses of associations serving as groups in your area, contact your state Blue Cross-Blue Shield organization. The address and phone number should be in your telephone directory, if not, ask any physician or medical group for the information.

# BUSINESS BROKERS

The number of business brokers who specialize in buying and selling businesses has proliferated and as the field has grown, so have clients' complaints, according to a recent report. There is little regulation and many deals are mishandled. The problem is that in most states business brokers, unlike real estate brokers, are not required to pass examinations or be licensed. Therefore caution in retaining a firm is urged. Check with your attorney, bank or the state real estate board before signing an agreement.

# BUSINESS CORRESPONDENCE

A large company has specialists in many departments to handle the various types of correspondence which are a necessary part of doing business. In the small business, however, the owner or his assistant must handle correspondence on every aspect of the business. The range of subjects is wide: sales, customer satisfaction, purchasing, contract negotiation, government regulations, taxes, product defects, discounts and special sales arrangements, unfair competition and collecting unpaid accounts.

It is helpful to have some guidance in the drafting of letters, and thus one or more of the books listed below may prove useful when correspondence problems arise. There cannot be a model letter to fit every situation, but one can always gain some insight from examples and ideas suggested by others.

**Suggested References**

Brusaw, Charles, et al, *The Business Writer's Handbook.* New York, St. Martin's Press, 1982.

Cypert, Samuel A., *Writing Effective Business Letters, Memos, Proposals and Reports.* Chicago, Contemporary Books, 1984.

DeVries, May A., *The Prentice-Hall Complete Secretarial Letter Book.* Englewood Cliffs, NJ, Prentice-Hall, 1978.

Gartside, I., *Model Business Letters.* Albuquerque, NM, Transatlantic, 1981.

*How to Write Better Business Letters.* Woodbury, NY, Barrons, 1982.

Leonard, Donald and Robert Shurter, *Effective Letters in Business.* New York, McGraw-Hill, 1984.

*Seventy Modern Business Letters.* Westbury, NY, Caddylak Publishing, 1983.

## BUSINESS DAY BOOK

Some of the most important records you may need for your business are not found in libraries or computer data bases, but are stored in your brain. Vital dates and telephone calls, names of visitors, and verbal agreements made in person or by phone are usually lost unless they are somehow recorded in a retrievable form. How often have you tried to recall an important date or conversation but been unable to do so?

The easiest way to establish such a running record is to obtain a small notebook which can be kept handy on your desk. It is not difficult to train yourself to jot down the name of each caller and the substance of the conversation together with brief notes regarding your outgoing calls and conversations. If you have a full-time secretary, she can keep a log of incoming and outgoing calls and the names of visitors, as well as such notations as you may give her regarding significant information you feel worth recording.

The outcome of a disagreement over dates or money matters, a need to reconstruct a sequence of events, or even the disposition of a lawsuit might well depend upon the information contained in the day book. Records of this type could prove well worth the small effort expended in keeping them from day to day.

## BUSINESS INFORMATION SOURCES

Frequently when one seeks specialized business information it is necessary to search beyond the resources of the local libraries. Fortunately there are several excellent reference books which should help and are available in most larger public, college and university libraries. Your librarian can probably tell you where you can locate these volumes, but if she cannot, contact your state library for help.

**Suggested References**

Brownstone, David, and Gorton Carruth, *Where to Find Business Information.* New York, John Wiley & Sons, 1982. The subject index lists over 2,500 subjects and refers to some 5,000 specialty business magazines, newspapers, and newsletters in this field.

*Books in Print* (Subject volumes). New York, R.R. Bowker, annual.

*Directory of Directories.* Information Research Enterprises, 1980– .

*Encyclopedia of Business Information Sources.* Detroit, Gale, 1983 (issued every 3–5 years). Arranged by topic under each are listed bibliographies, biographical sources, dictionaries, encyclopedias, handbooks, indexes, manuals, periodicals, statistical sources, etc.

*Reader's Guide to Periodical Literature.* New York, H.W. Wilson, cumulates, 1900– . This indexes about 180 periodicals, many of them carrying articles of interest to those in business.

## BUSINESS PUBLICATIONS

There are literally scores of business periodicals and newspapers; many of them cover the news and developments of a single industry. Here we list some of the better known magazines which should be of interest to most businessmen. A few of these publications are focused on small business as indicated by their titles. Send for a sample copy of any which interest you. Be prepared to pay for it although there may be no charge.

*Better Business*, National Minority Business Council, Inc., 235 East 42 Street, New York, NY 10017. Quarterly. (Covers small/minority business.)

*Business Age, The Magazine for Small Business*, PO Box 11597, Milwaukee, WI 53211. Bimonthly.

*Business Today*, PO Box 10010, Ogden, UT, 84409. Monthly.

*Business Week*, 1221 Avenue of the Americas, New York, 10020. Weekly.

*Communication Briefings*, 806 Westminster Road, Blackwood, NJ 08012. Monthly newsletter. (Practical ideas on improving business techniques and management.)

*D & B Reports, The Dun & Bradstreet Magazine for Small Business Management*, 299 Park Avenue, New York, NY 10170. Bimonthly.

*The Executive Female*, 1041 Third Avenue, New York, NY 10021. Bimonthly.

*Fortune*, Time & Life Building, Rockefeller Center, New York, NY 10020. Biweekly.

*Home Business News, The Magazine for Home-Based Entrepreneurs*, 12221 Beaver Pike, Jackson, OH 45640. Bimonthly.

*May Trends*, George S. May International Company, Park Ridge, IL 60068. Three times a year. (For owner's and managers of small and medium sized businesses.)

*INC Magazine, The Magazine for Growing Companies*, 38 Commercial Wharf, Boston, MA 02110. Monthly.

*Sales and Marketing Management*, Bill Communications Inc., 633 Third Avenue, New York, NY 10017. Monthly.

*Stop Line, An Executive Briefing Service*, 505 Market Street, Knoxville, TN 37902. Quarterly. (Covers business management for owners and chief executive officers of small and medium sized companies.)

## BUSINESS PUBLICATIONS (continued)

*Venture, The Magazine for Entrepreneurs*, 521 Fifth Avenue, New York, NY 10175. Monthly. **Note:** For a complete directory of all newspapers and periodicals see the *Gale Directory of Publications*, Detroit, Gale, annual. This was formerly titled *Ayers Directory*.

## BUSINESS WOMEN'S ASSOCIATION

Membership in the American Business Women's Association is open to all women who are employed in business; annual national dues are $35. There are more than 112,000 members and 2,100 chapters throughout the United States and Puerto Rico. The Association brings together business women of diverse backgrounds and provides opportunities for them to help themselves and others grow personally and professionally through leadership, education, networking support and national recognition. Members are employed in nearly all fields and job levels.

**For Further Information**

American Business Women's Association
9100 Ward Parkway
Kansas City, MO 64114-0728
Phone: 816-361-6621

## BUYING OR SELLING A BUSINESS

Although almost 10,000 firms are bought and sold every day of the work week, most small business owners have few if any guidelines to help them come up with the right price when they decide to sell their businesses or acquire other firms. Although the traditional yardstick of real business worth is the value of the net assets plus as much as three times the net profit, there are many other factors that should be taken into consideration.

If you are considering the sale of your business or the purchase of another, you can ask your banker, attorney or accountant to let you know of any prospects. Another way is to use the services of a broker who specializes in buying and selling business properties. Most brokers work for a percentage fee of up to 10 percent of the selling price of the property, although that may be negotiable. Alternatively, a broker may agree to work on a flat fee basis as a consultant.

The Institute of Certified Business Counselors is a non-profit trade association comprised of brokers, salespersons, consultants, accountants, attorneys, appraisers and business owners interested in the continuation, valuation or buying and selling of businesses for their own account or for a fee. After approval for membership, certification requires taking certain home study courses and passing examinations. Thus a degree of professionalism is assured if one retains a business counselor who is a member of this organization. Members agree to abide by a code of ethics adopted by the Institute's board of directors.

**For Further Information**

Institute of Certified Business Counselors
PO Box 30695
Walnut Creek, CA 94598
Phone: 415-945-8440

**Suggested References**

Pratt, Shannon P., *Valuing Small Businesses and Professional Practices.* Portland, OR, Willamette Management Associates, Inc.

—— *Valuing a Business: The Analysis and Appraisal of Closely-Held Companies.* Portland, OR, Willamette Management Associates.

# CENSUS

Because of its importance to every businessman, the activities of the Bureau of the Census are given in some detail.

The Bureau of the Census is a general purpose statistical agency which collects, tabulates, and publishes a wide variety of statistical data about the nation's people and the economy. These data are used by Congress, the executive branch and the public in the development and evaluation of economic and social programs. The constitution authorized the Bureau to take a census of population every ten years but in addition to this, the principal functions of the Bureau include the following:

Decennial (10) censuses of population and housing; quinquennial (5) censuses of agriculture, state and local governments, manufacturers, mineral industries, distributive trades, construction industries, and transportation; current surveys that provide information on many of the subjects covered in the censuses at monthly, quarterly, annual or other intervals; and compilations of current statistics on U.S., foreign trade, including data on imports, exports and shipping.

In addition, the Bureau conducts special censuses at the request and expense of states and local governmental units; publishes estimates and projections of the population; provides current data on population and housing characteristics; and issues current reports on manufacturing, retail and wholesale trade, services, construction, imports and exports, state and local government finances and employment, and other subjects.

"The Monthly Product Announcement" (the term product refers to the publications issued by the Bureau) lists new publications under headings such as: Agriculture, Economic, General and Reference, Governments, Housing, Maps, Population, Population and Housing, Technical Documentation, and Data Files. Those interested in the wide range of Bureau publications should subscribe to the "Monthly Product Announcement" which is issued free of charge. To obtain a subscription, write to Data User Services Division, Customer Services, Bureau of the Census, Washington, DC 20233.

# CENSUS (continued)

## For Further Information

Bureau of the Census
Washington, DC 20233
Phone: 301-763-4100

## CENTER FOR FAMILY BUSINESS

The Center for Family Business is an organization serving business owners and their families headed by Dr. Leon A. Danco who holds degrees from Harvard and the Harvard Business School, and a Ph.D. from Case Western Reserve University. The principal activity of the Center is holding family business seminars. Titles of the 1986–1987 seminar held in Cleveland was "Managing Succession Without Conflict," and for a seven-day program held in Hawaii, "Planning for the Future as a Business Owning Family."

### For Further Information

The Center for Family Business
PO Box 24268
Cleveland, OH 44124
Phone: 216-442-0800

### Suggested References

Dr. Danco is the author of the following books which are obtainable from the Center: *Beyond Survival, Inside the Family Business,* and *Outside Directors in the Family Owned Business.*

## CHAMBERS OF COMMERCE

Chambers of Commerce will be found in over 7,000 cities and towns throughout the United States. In addition there are many other chambers which represent foreign nations. The objects of the Littleton Chamber of Commerce, one of New Hampshire's more aggressive and forward-looking chambers, give a good idea of the purposes of a chamber. Following are excerpts from the by laws of that group:

"The objects of this association are to secure a union of the energies, influence and action of citizens in all matters pertaining to the moral and material welfare of Littleton . . . to encourage all legitimate business enterprises; to disseminate through the press and otherwise, information relative to the advantages of Littleton as a field for industrial activities and a place of residence . . . to promote the prosperity, comfort and general well-being of all our citizens; to stimulate civic pride and progress; and, in short, make a bigger, better and busier Littleton."

As the above indicates, chambers are service-oriented groups, providing all types of information to their members, the public at large, travelers and tourists, business interests, and those who request specialized data. Thus they serve as an excellent research source for all types of information about communities or areas. When data is needed about another city or town, start your research by contacting that chamber of commerce. If you do not know the address, send your request to the Chamber of Commerce, care of the Postmaster.

### Suggested Reference

*World Wide Chamber of Commerce Directory.* Boulder, CO, Johnson Publishing Co., annual.

## CHARITABLE SOLICITATIONS

Every business, regardless of size, is asked to contribute to various charitable and non-profit organizations ranging from local Girl Scout troops to capital campaigns of colleges. Large companies may have an individual whose sole duty is to evaluate donation requests and administer the contributions and membership budgets. In smaller firms the owner may assume the job or delegate it to another employee. Because of the demands made on many companies and the new concept of corporate social responsibility, this activity is an important and sensitive one.

Perhaps the small businessman faces the most difficult decision because he is beseiged by every organization in town. If he can draw up a giving policy defining what he will and will not support and stick to it, that is his best defense for saying no. When it comes to those organizations which are not purely local but are affiliated with a county, state or national movement, he may want to obtain information that will enable him to determine whether or not it deserves his support.

Some counties and cities maintain records on certain non-profit organizations. In areas where this is done, such files may be consulted or information obtained by telephone. Contact the Office of Consumer Affairs or the city or county clerk's office for information. Some local Better Business Bureaus and Chambers of Commerce also maintain active solicitation files and will give current data on local charitable groups. Consult the phone directory for their addresses and phone numbers.

If you receive numerous solicitations from national groups you may be interested in the National Charities Information Bureau which was founded in 1918. This is a non-profit investigating organization which prepares confidential reports for its members and provides advisory services, not on local, but on national and international fund-raising nonprofit organizations in many fields. Each report gives information on the agency's purpose, program, finances and leadership in terms of eight basic standards.

An institutional contribution of $100 provides a one-year subscription to the Wise Giving Guide, unlimited access to full reports, and response to telephone inquiries as needed. Remembering that reports are on national groups, these services

## CHARITABLE SOLICITATIONS (continued)

can be enormously helpful to small and medium sized companies as well as more than 4,000 individuals support the NCIB.

The Foundation Center is an educational organization which collects and disseminates information about foundations, their purpose, and grants. It makes available published reports and information, maintains a library of books, articles, and pamphlets, as well as bound volumes of annual foundation reports. There are branch research libraries also in Cleveland, San Francisco, and Washington, D.C. plus numerous cooperating collections. There is no charge for using the libraries or asking questions.

### For Further Information

National Charities Information Bureau
19 Union Square West
New York, NY 10003
Phone: 212-929-6300

Foundation Center
79 Fifth Avenue
New York, NY 10003
Phone: 212-620-4230

### Suggested References

Dermer, Joseph and Stephen Wertheimer, editors, *The Complete Guide to Corporate Fund Raising.* Arlington, VA, Volunteer, The National Center for Citizen Involvement, 1982.

Podesta, Aldo, *Raising Funds from America's Two Million Overlooked Corporations.* Hartsdale, NY, Public Service Materials Center, 1984.

**Note:** Inquiries addressed to either of the two organizations listed above may obtain the names of additional books, especially those which treat company giving.

# CIVIL RIGHTS

The Civil Rights Act of 1964 aimed to eliminate employment discrimination based on color, sex, and religion in industries engaged in interstate commerce. After its fourth year the law covered employers of at least 25 workers.

The act established the Equal Employment Opportunity Commission (EEOC) to administer and enforce the fair employment practice sections of the statute, although it was not given power to conduct enforcement. In 1972 a new act, the Equal Employment Opportunity Act was adopted which gave the EEOC authority to take to court complaints of discrimination on the basis of race, religion or sex which could not be resolved under mediation or conciliation.

Since July 1, 1979 the EEOC has had responsibility for enforcing the Equal Pay Act of 1963 and the Age Discrimination in Employment Act of 1967. The former law prohibits sex-based pay differences where work performed under similar working conditions is of equal skill, effort and responsibility. The latter law prohibits employment discrimination against workers or applicants 40–70 years of age.

A significant activity of the EEOC is its Voluntary Assistance Program designed to provide educational and technical assistance to small and midsize employers and unions through one-day seminars on equal employment opportunity laws about their rights and obligations under all the statutes that the Commission enforces.

## For Further Information

Equal Employment Opportunity Commission
Washington, DC 20507
A toll-free number puts callers in touch with a tape bank where information about EEOC programs and activities may be acquired and the caller directed to the proper EEOC field office. This number is 800-USA-EEOC. For more general information call 202-634-6922.

## Suggested References

*Guidebook to Fair Employment Practices.* Chicago, Commerce Clearing House, 1983.

# CIVIL RIGHTS (continued)

Peres, Richard, *Preventing Discrimination Complaints: A Guide for Supervisors.* New York, McGraw-Hill, 1979.

*Understanding EEO: A Supervisor's Casebook.* New York, Executive Enterprises, 1974.

# COLLECTION AGENCIES

One serious problem shared by most businesses is the account receivable which is difficult if not impossible to collect. Most small claims courts will consider suits of $100 or less. For accounts larger than this amount it is necessary to use the services of your attorney or those of a collection agency. Most agencies charge fees ranging from 30 to 50 percent of the amount collected. See the yellow pages of your phone book for local agencies listed under the heading: "Collection Agencies," or contact the local or state Chamber of Commerce for a list of collection agencies from which you may choose one to service your account. Your bank or attorney may also be able to refer you to a reputable firm.

The organization listed below represents some 3,200 collection offices throughout the world, serving over 1 million professional, retail and wholesale credit grantors.

**For Further Information**

American Collectors Association, Inc.
PO Box 35106
Minneapolis, MN 55435
Phone: 612-926-6547

**See also:** CREDIT MANAGEMENT.

# COMMODITIES, FUTURES, AND OPTIONS EXCHANGES

For the convenience of readers who may wish to contact one of these exchanges, the addresses and phone numbers of the principal exchanges are given below.

**For Further Information**

Board of Trade of Kansas City
4800 Main Street
Kansas City, MO 64112-2510
Phone: 816-753-1101

Chicago Board Options Exchange
141 West Jackson Boulevard
Chicago, IL 60604-2904
Phone: 312-431-5600

Chicago Board of Trade
141 West Jackson Boulevard
Chicago, IL 60604-2904
Phone: 312-435-3500

Chicago Mercantile Exchange
175 West Jackson Boulevard
Chicago, IL 60604-2601
Phone: 312-435-0606

Coffee, Sugar, and Cocoa Exchange
4 World Trade Center
New York, NY 10048
Phone: 212-938-2800

Commodity Exchange
4 World Trade Center
New York, NY 10048-0204
Phone: 212-938-2000

Mid-America Commodity Exchange
175 West Jackson Boulevard
Chicago, IL 60604-2601
Phone: 312-435-0606

Minneapolis Grain Exchange
400 South 4th Street
Minneapolis, MN 55415-1410
Phone: 612-338-6212

New Orleans Commodity Exchange
308 Board of Trade Place
New Orleans, LA 70130
Phone: 504-524-2184

New York Cotton Exchange
4 World Trade Center
New York, NY 10048-0201
Phone: 212-938-2650

## COMMODITIES, FUTURES, AND OPTIONS EXCHANGES

(continued)

New York Futures Exchange
30 Broad Street
New York, NY 10004-2304
Phone: 212-820-7000

New York Mercantile Exchange
4 World Trade Center
New York, NY 10048-0204
Phone: 212-938-2222

## COMPUTERS

Although computers can be effective they are not a panacea for all small business operations. Often vendors sell equipment when it is not needed. Before you purchase a computer, make certain you really need one. Retain a qualified consultant to analyze your needs.

We know of one small businessman who thought that a modest size computer to keep his records, together with a word processor to handle his correspondence, would make a very worthwhile investment. A year after installing the system he found that he was better off before he made his purchase. When he tried to sell his equipment, there was little interest because by that time his investment had become obsolete.

If you have decided to purchase a computer, there are two ways to go about this:

1. Learn about them yourself. This calls for an investment of time and possibly attending classes at a vocational/technical school or community college.

2. Retain a consultant to advise you about your possible computer requirements. Beware of a consultant who sells equipment; it might be preferable to find a fully independent consultant who only recomends what to buy.

As for sources of supply:

1. There are vendors who can package a system to meet your needs. It may be costly but you should receive good service.

2. You can have a consultant purchase equipment, as mentioned above.

3. You can save more money by purchasing through mail order, but you must be cautious and you really should know what you are doing. Be sure of the guarantee you will receive; it should be a 30-day money back guarantee with a one year guarantee on performance. There should also be a toll-free number for inquiries in case you need assistance in setting it up or operating it. Check the conditions for return.

When you investigate systems, consider one which meets industry standards. Since the market changes rapidly, make sure you can use other software with what you are considering. IBM compatible is the present industry standard, and most software is written for this model. Most manufacturers are getting into the IBM standard, but find out if the product you are buying is standard.

## COMPUTERS (continued)

Should you live in a rural area and cannot or prefer not to obtain the advice of a consultant, look at the yellow pages of the phone book for listings of computer dealers. Your best course of action may be to take the word-of-mouth advice of friends or business associates who have purchased computers which they found satisfactory.

**For Further Information**

Computer and Business Equipment
    Manufacturers Association
311 First Street NW
Washington, DC 20001

**Suggested References**

Bradbeer, Robin, et al, *The Beginner's Guide to Computers.* Reading, MA, Addison-Wesley, 1983.

Byers, Robert, *Everyman's Database Primer.* Culver City, CA, Ashton-Tate Books.

Graham, Neil, *Introduction to Computer Science: A Structured Approach.* St. Paul, MN, West Publishing, 1982.

McWilliams, Peter A., *The Personal Computer in Business Book.* New York, Random House, 1983.

*PC Magazine: The Independent Guide to IBM Standard Personal Computing.* New York, Ziff Communication Co., bi-weekly.

*PC World.* San Francisco, PCW Communications, Inc., monthly. (Contains reviews of hardware and software; the advertising of numerous mail order houses is one of its greatest benefits.)

## CONCILIATION

A conciliator in labor disputes brings parties together and urges them to agree to any solutions which are freely offered by both sides, but he cannot exert any binding force on the disputing parties. The Federal Mediation and Conciliation Service helps prevent disruptions in interstate commerce caused by labor-management disputes by providing mediators to help disputing parties resolve their differences.

**For Further Information**

Office of Information and Public Affairs
Federal Mediation and Conciliation Service
2100 K Street, NW
Washington, DC 20427
Phone: 202-653-5290

**Note:** For disputes which do not involve interstate commerce, contact the Labor Department at your state capital

**See also:** ARBITRATION, MEDIATION

# CONSUMER COMPLAINTS

If you buy from a door-to-door salesman or order from a catalog by mail, you have certain protections under the law.

## Door-to-Door Sales

Federal Trade Commission rules make it mandatory for salesmen of goods or services worth $25 or more to tell you about your cancellation rights (the "Cooling Off Rule"), and the sales contract must contain information about your right to cancel. Remember, however, that if you wish to exercise this option, you must do so within three business days. The rule does not apply to phone or mail sales; sales under $25; sales of insurance, real estate, or securities; sales made in a store; emergency repairs if you waive the right to cancel; or maintenance or repair of your property if you initiated the sale.

If you have a complaint about the "Cooling off Rule," write the Federal Trade Commission, Washington, DC 20580. For other complaints contact the local, county, or state consumer protection office, or the state Attorney General's office at the state capitol. Look in the phone book for the phone numbers under the appropriate government heading.

## Mail Order Sales

The seller must ship your order no later than 30 days after your order arrives. If the seller is unable to do this, he must inform you and give you the option of canceling and receiving a prompt refund. Upon receiving notification that you want a refund, the company must pay it within seven days, or adjust your account within one billing cycle if you paid by credit card. This rule does not apply if you used a toll free number to order and charged the purchase to your credit card.

If you have a complaint about the product, your refund or anything else to do with the order, write the company and send carbon copies to the U.S. Postal Service, Washington, DC 20260, the Federal Trade Commission, Washington, DC 20580, and any pertinent organizations which you feel would want to know about the problem.

Should you have a complaint against a national bank (not state), contact the bank's consumer

## CONSUMER COMPLAINTS (continued)

complaint representative or department and try to resolve the complaint. If the bank fails to solve the problem, obtain a complaint form from the bank (Comptroller of the Currency form CC9050-08) and mail it to the National Bank Region for your state at the address listed on the form.

# CONSUMER INFORMATION

In 1970 the Consumer Information Center was established by the federal government to help agencies promote and distribute useful consumer information. A new *Consumer Information Catalog* is published quarterly, representing the best new federal consumer booklets. These low priced publications are available only through the Consumer Information Center and the catalogs include prices of all booklets.

Contents of a typical issue include the following subjects: Careers and Education, Children, Federal Benefits, Food, Health, Housing, Money Management, Small Business, Travel and Hobbies, Miscellaneous, and Sources of Assistance.

Request a copy of the latest *Consumer Information Catalog* from Consumer Information Center, Pueblo, CO 81009.

# CONSUMER PRODUCT SAFETY

The Consumer Product Safety Commission is responsible for enforcing the provisions of the Consumer Product Safety Act, the Flammable Fabrics Act, the Poison Prevention Packaging Act, the Federal Hazardous Substances Act and the act prohibiting transportation of refrigerators without door safety devices.

The Commission requires manufacturers to report defects in products that would create substantial hazards; requires corrective action where hazardous products are already in commerce; collects information on consumer product-related injuries and maintains an injury information clearinghouse; conducts research on product hazards; assists in developing safety standards; establishes mandatory consumer product standards; and bans products where appropriate.

**For Further Information**

Office of Information and Public Affairs
Consumer Product Safety Commission
1111-18th Street, NW
Washington, DC 20207
Phone 301-492-6580
A public information room is maintained at the above address. A toll-free Consumer Product Safety Hotline is available: 800-638-CPSC, plus a teletypewriter for the hearing-impaired at 800-638-8270 (in Maryland only, 800-492-8104).

# CONVENTIONS

There is a growing trend within American business to meet, exchange information and expertise and fraternize at conventions. Although many are held at posh resorts with much time devoted to recreation, there is little doubt that conventions serve a purpose in giving management members and specialists opportunity to become better acquainted and profit from an exchange of information.

## For Further Information

International Association of Convention and Visitors Bureaus
PO Box 758
Champaign, IL 61820
This association acts in the capacity of a clearinghouse for convention information and dates.

# COPYRIGHT

Works subject to copyrighting and copyright renewal include books, periodicals, dramatic and musical compositions, maps, works of art and reproductions of a work of art, photographs, prints, or labels used for articles of merchandise, motion pictures and sound recordings. The Library of Congress is responsible for the business of copyrighting which is carried on through its Copyright Office. The fee is $10 per item.

Under the new law, writing is protected as soon as it is put on paper with protection lasting for the life of the author plus 50 years. This applies if the work is written or registered with the Copyright Office after January 1, 1978. Registration gives certain advantages, especially if an infringement case is brought to court.

## For Further Information

Copyright Office
Library of Congress
101 Independence Avenue, SE.
Washington, DC 20559
Phone: 202-287-5000
Upon request the Copyright Office will send all the information needed to prepare a copyright application, including application forms. Registration application forms may be ordered by calling Forms Hotline at 202-287-9100.

## Suggested References

*Corporate Copyrights and Information Practices*, #C02089, Law and Business. New York, Harcourt, Brace, Jovanovich.

Heller, James S. and Sarah K. Wiant, *Copyright Handbook.* (AALL Publications Set: No. 23). Littleton, CO, Fred B. Rothman & Co., 1984.

# CORPORATION–ADVANTAGES

There are several advantages to the corporate form of organization. The most important is the company's ability to sell shares of stock to the public to raise capital for expansion. This, in turn, enables the public to invest its savings in American business and participate in its growth and profits. Another advantage is the limited liability which a corporation enjoys with respect to any debts. Only the corporation—not its stockholders—is liable for its obligations, and in the event of bankruptcy, the stockholders are not endangered. In the case of a proprietorship or partnership, the owners are personally liable for all debts.

A corporation has a continuous life and does not cease operation because an officer or director dies or sells his interest. The corporate organization also permits ownership of its shares to be transferred from one person to another. This can be done easily and quickly if the stock is listed on a national or regional stock exchange.

**See also:** FORMS OF BUSINESS ORGANIZATIONS, INCORPORATING A BUSINESS

# CORPORATE AFFILIATIONS

With the merger madness that has infected the corporate world of business, it is difficult to know who owns whom in the tangled web of corporate linkage. Should you be approached by a company interested in purchasing your business, or should you be interested in acquiring an established company, you would want to know its background and whether it is independently owned or a subsidiary of a parent corporation.

You can investigate (1) by obtaining a Dun & Bradstreet report, possibly through your bank, accountant, or attorney; or (2) by consulting an expensive directory which gives corporate affiliations such as those listed below.

**Suggested References**

*Directory of Corporate Affiliations.* Wilmette, IL, Directory of Corporate Affiliations, 1987.

Lovejoy, Frederick A., ed., *The Princeton Mergers and Acquisitions Reporter and Directory* (5 volumes). Princeton, NJ, Princeton Research Institute, 1981

*Who Owns Whom, North America.* New York, Dun & Bradstreet, 1986.

# CORPORATE INFORMATION

There are several standard reference works which give excellent information about corporations: names and affiliations of directors and officers, capsulated corporate history, financial data and operating statistics. The services vary in the extent and nature of their coverage, and because of their size, are generally purchased only by larger libraries.

## Suggested References

*Corporation Records.* New York, Standard and Poor's, annual (7 volumes).

*Million Dollar Directory: Top 50,000 Companies.* New York, Dun & Bradstreet, 1987 (7 volumes).

*Moody's Industrial Manual.* New York, Moody's Investors Service, current looseleaf and annual. (Also publishes: *Moody's Bank and Finance Manual, Moody's Municipal and Government Manual, Moody's International Manual, Moody's Public Utility Manual,* and *Moody's Transportation Manual.*)

*Reference Book of Corporate Managements: American Corporate Leaders.* New York, Dun & Bradstreet. (4 volumes)

# CORPORATE SECRETARY FUNCTIONS

The corporate secretary has certain responsibilities which are stated in the corporate bylaws as well as those generally dictated by statute or government regulations. The scope of responsibilities varies from company to company but they basically entail handling details pertaining to the directors' and stockholders' meetings, maintaining the records of company securities, as well as other records, licenses, permits, contracts, agreements, etc.

## For Further Information

American Society of Corporate Secretaries
1270 Avenue of the Americas
New York, NY 10020
Phone: 212-765-2620

Membership of this association consists of secretaries, assistant secretaries, officers and executives of corporations who are concerned with corporate practices and procedures. The society conducts various surveys and compiles statistics, operates a placement service, issues special reports and holds an annual convention. The special reports which are available to members cover many of the secretary's duties and responsibilities.

## Suggested Reference

Kozoll, Charles E., *Executive Secretary: Functions and Responsibilities.* Cranford, NJ, Didactic Systems, 1975.

# COST OF LIVING

The various consumer and producer price indexes compiled and published by the Bureau of Labor Statistics of the U. S. Department of Labor are the most authoritative and complete statistics measuring the cost of living. In addition the Bureau compiles data on consumer expenditures and family budgets. These figures are averaged by geographical area, product, and service.

## For Further Information

Bureau of Labor Statistics
U.S. Department of Labor
Washington, DC 20210

## Suggested Reference

Both the *World Almanac* and the *Information Please Almanac* contain selected consumer price indexes but more complete tables will be found in the *Statistical Abstract of the United States.* Data in the latter are not current and those in the almanacs are usually a year or two behind. Bureau of Labor Statistics, *Consumer Price Index— Detailed Report.* Washington, Superintendent of Documents, monthly.

——*CPI Detailed Report.* Washington, Superintendent of Documents, annual.

**Note:** A recorded summary of principal current Consumer Price Indexes, Producer Price Indexes, and Employment Situation numbers is available 24 hours a day by calling 202-523-9658.

# CREDIT CARD INTEREST RATES

Whether you have one or more bank credit cards or thinking of applying for one, you should pay attention to the interest rates charged for your unpaid balance. Here are three points many banks neglect to tell their subscribers:

1. More and more banks are using different rates (referred to as tiered rates) for different types of customers. If you run a high monthly balance or have multiple accounts in your bank, your interest rate may be lower than that of other cardholders who have fewer accounts.

2. In 1987 there was a movement toward adopting variable rates which reflect the prime rate (the interest rate which the Federal Reserve Bank charges commercial banks for borrowing). One commercial bank charged six percentage points over the prime rate for a regular Visa card. Another bank charged nine percentage points over the rate it paid on its three-month certificates of deposit. A third institution charged twice the rate of a six-month Treasury Bill or 14 percent, whichever was higher. Customers who run sizable balances tend to be better off with variable rates, but it is something which should be investigated.

3. Usually cardholders have had a 25-day grace period after receiving their statements to pay their bills before interest was charged. Many banks, however, have dropped the grace period and charge interest for late payment.

It pays to visit the bank and check on the latest bank card regulations so you can plan your payments and avoid unnecessary interest.

## Suggested References

Nelson, Tom and Bruce Brown, *The Complete Credit Book: How to Get a Visa or MasterCard With no Credit Check.* Los Angeles, Inflation Reports, 1984.

Pollan, Stephen and Raymond Roel, *How to Borrow Money.* New York, Cornerstone, 1983.

## CREDIT CARDS FOR MERCHANTS

A small business which wishes to give its customers the convenience of charging purchases or services on Master Charge or Visa, should request an application blank from its bank. There is a $50 non-refundable application fee to cover investigation and processing. Monthly charges are assessed based on the average amount of individual sales and the monthly volume. There is no minimum volume requirement.

## CREDIT MANAGEMENT

The National Association of Credit Management (NACM) was founded June 23, 1896 in Toledo; membership has since grown to over 44,000, making it the oldest and largest business organization in the United States. NACM members are business credit grantors in manufacturing, wholesaling, service industries and financial institutions. Members are served by some 75 autonomous affiliated state and regional associations throughout the country.

One of its most important services is providing credit reports that offer members fast, accurate, current and objective information minutes after the request for credit is received. Information in the NACM automated files is supplied by a broad spectrum of local, regional and national firms.

For men and women in the same field of business, NACM also provides an opportunity to participate regularly in informative round table discussions of accounts as well as mutual concerns. Credit groups operate in virtually every industry, and more than 1,500 industry credit groups are sponsored and operated by affiliated associations.

Other activities include a collection service, numerous publications, a monthly magazine and opportunity to qualify for accreditation as an Accredited Business Credit Executive.

**For Further Information**

National Association of Credit Management
520 Eighth Avenue
New York, NY 10018-6571
Phone: 212-947-5070

**See also:** COLLECTION AGENCIES

# CREDIT UNIONS

Credit Unions date back to 1849 and today are big business with almost 20,000 credit unions serving some 40 million members. The largest number serve employees of companies and government. Credit unions are owned and operated by their members who make their savings available for low cost loans to all the members. Many employers have found that a credit union helps their company because it contributes to the financial well-being of its employees. Payroll deduction provides not only a regular means of saving but also a way of repaying loans.

## For Further Information

Credit Union National Association
P.O. Box 431
Madison, WI 53701
Phone: 608-231-4000

# CRIME

Crime can attack the businessman internally and externally. Shoplifting and employee theft can cut profits and create difficult problems. Forced entry, vandalism and other forms of crime from the street can become even greater problems. Citizens watching for crime and reporting it to the law enforcement agency have successfully reduced crime in many areas. If crime is rampant in your city or town you can help reduce it with the help of National Crime Prevention Council community action kits and other helpful materials.

In the plant, the job is mostly your responsibility. Don't overlook the local Chamber of Commerce or Better Business Bureau as resources for help and information. Perhaps one or more of the books listed below will prove helpful. Your library may have others or be able to refer you to organizations that can assist you.

## For Further Information

National Crime Prevention Council
733 15th Street, NW
Washington, DC 20005
Phone: 202-393-7141

## Suggested References

Council of Better Business Bureaus, *How To Protect Your Business.* Arlington, VA, Council of Better Business Bureaus.

Nader, L. R., *Protecting Your Business Against Employee Thefts, Shoplifters and Other Hazards.* New York, Pilot Books, 1977.

Post, Richard S., editor, *Combatting Crime Against Small Business.* Springfield, IL, C.C. Thomas Publisher, 1972.

The U.S. Justice Department's Office of Justice Programs for the Crime Prevention Coalition, has published some 15 booklets roughly 20 pages in length and covering specific types of crime and potential victims. Titles of interest to businessmen include: "Got a Minute? You Could Stop A Crime.", "Arson—How Not To Get Burned.", "How To Protect Your Neighborhood.", "How Not To Get Conned.", "How To Crimeproof Your Business.", "How Your Organization Can Take Action Against Crime.", "How To Prevent Rural

## CRIME (continued)

Crime.". Individual copies are available at no charge from: Crime Prevention Coalition, McGruff Campaign, PO Box 6600, Rockville, MD 20850.

**See also:** SHOPLIFTING

## CURRENT AND PAST EVENTS

Frequently it is necessary to look up a newsworthy event to establish a date, or for some other reason, but it may be difficult to locate it or remember when it occurred. There are a few good reference books which make it possible to locate important dates and events.

For recent years since 1941 *Facts on File* is the best, provided your local library subscribes to it. This weekly summary of national and international news events covers a wide range of subjects from agriculture and the arts to banking, economics, and law. It has a most useful cumulative index. Both the *World Almanac* and the *Information Please Almanac* contain chronologies, that of the latter going back before Christ. The *Cyclopedia of Classified Dates* is a compilation of events of all types from prehistory to 1900, as is the *People's Chronology: A Year-by-Year Record of Human Events from Prehistory to the Present*. The *New York Times Index* is useful too.

Your best procedure is to tell the reference librarian what you are seeking and then work with whatever almanacs and chronologies the library may have on hand. If it does not have any of the books listed below, perhaps the librarian can contact a larger library or the state library and ask the reference librarian there to look up the information.

### Suggested References

*Cyclopedia of Classified Dates.* Detroit, Gale Research, 1967 (original published in 1900).

*Facts on File: Weekly World News Digest with Cumulative Index.* New York, Facts on File, current.

*Information Please Almanac.* Boston, Houghton Mifflin, annual.

*New York Times Index.* New York, New York Times, monthly.

*People's Chronology; A Year-by-Year Record of Human Events from Prehistory to the Present.* New York, Holt, Rinehart and Winston, 1979.

*The World Almanac and Book of Facts.* New York, Pharos Books, annual.

# DEPRECIATION

There is no single, generally accepted definition of the word "depreciation." Accountants, economists, engineers, lawyers, tax experts and others have constructed different meanings, each to meet their particular requirements. Perhaps the American Institute of Certified Public Accountants' definition will suffice for our purposes:

"Depreciation accounting is a system of accounting which aims to distribute the cost or other basic value of tangible capital assets, less salvage (if any), over the estimated useful life of the unit (which may be a group of assets) in a systematic and rational manner. It is a process of allocation, not of valuation. Depreciation for the year is the portion of the total charge under such a system that is allocated to the year."

Depreciation, as in the case of an airline which is depreciating several multimillion dollar airplanes, will generate a great deal of cash and thereby reduce profits—and income taxes as well. In the case of a small business, there may be little other than office equipment and specialized machines to give depreciation treatment, but it is an accounting device which should not be overlooked and must be reviewed with one's lawyer and tax accountant.

**Suggested References**

Baxter, W., *Depreciating Assets*. New York, Van Nostrand Reinhold, 1981.

Coughlan, Joseph D. and William K. Strand, *Depreciation: Accounting, Taxes, and Business Decisions*. Ann Arbor, MI, Books on Demand.

Johnson, James M., *Handbook of Depreciation Methods, Formulas and Tables*. Englewood Cliffs, NJ, Prentice-Hall, 1982.

*The New ABC's of the Depreciation and Investment Credit*. Englewood Cliffs, NJ, Prentice-Hall, 1983.

Saliers, Earl A., *Principles of Depreciation*. Salem, NH, Ayer Co., 1981.

# DEPRESSIONS

The United States has suffered depressions of varying degrees during the following years:

| | | |
|---|---|---|
| 1785-1789 | 1857 | 1893-1895 |
| 1808-1809 | 1860-1861 | 1903-1904 |
| 1814 | 1868-1869 | 1907-1908 |
| 1819-1820 | 1873-1875 | 1914 |
| 1825 | 1878 | 1920-1921 |
| 1837-1839 | 1884 | 1930-1940 |
| 1847-1848 | 1889-1890 | |

An economic decline which is milder than a depression is referred to as a recession. At such times thousands or even millions may be unemployed and business activity may drop drastically, but the decline is short and the economy as a whole is not badly hurt. There have been several periods of recession since 1940 but none sufficiently severe to be classified as a depression.

Readers interested in reading further on the subject may find the following books of interest.

**Suggested References**

Bird, Caroline, *The Invisible Scar*. New York, David McKay, 1966. (The 1930-1940 depression)

Galbraith, John Kenneth, *The Great Crash: 1929*. Princeton, NJ, Princeton University Press, 1963.

Lightner, Otto C., *History of Business Depressions: A Vivid Portrayal of Periods of Economic Adversity from the Beginning of Commerce to the Present*. New York, Franklin, Burt, Publishing, 1970.

Morine, John, *Riding the Recession*. Brookfield, VT, Brookfield Publishing, 1981.

Neilson, Francis, *Pertinent Lessons from Past Depressions*. Brooklyn, NY, Revisionist Press, 1979.

Warren, Harris Gaylord, *Herbert Hoover and the Great Depression*. New York, Oxford University Press, 1959.

# DISABLED EMPLOYEES

Mainstream, Inc. is a national non-profit organization that provides employers, educational institutions and community organizations with information, training, and technical assistance on diverse disability issues. Its goal is to enhance the successful mainstreaming of disabled people into American society.

Employers interested in employing disabled applicants will find this organization publishes much helpful literature. It has also been operating a job level and placement service (LINK) for disabled individuals, and has experienced a 90 percent job retention record for those placed in the initial two cities, Dallas and Washington, DC. Its clients have included a number of public, private and non-profit organizations.

Write for a copy of the Mainstream Publications Catalog and address all inquiries to the address listed below.

## For Further Information

Mainstream, Inc.
1200 15th Street, NW
Washington, DC 20005
Phone: 202-833-1136
Voice/TDD

# DISTRIBUTION

Distribution is an all-embracing term which usually refers to the shipping out and sale of a company's products. Without distribution it is impossible to sell one's products. Here are some of the major activities associated with distribution: selling, shipping, storage, financing, collecting, and reviewing marketing information. Obviously this is a function which the manufacturer—large or small—must resolve satisfactorily. The alternative is business failure.

Each business has its own distribution problems peculiar to itself. However, there are both theoretical and practical principles applicable to all businesses which are discussed in the books listed below, as well as in many general accounting handbooks.

## Suggested References

Christopher, Martin, et al, *Customer Service and Distribution Strategy.* New York, Halsted Press, 1980.

Higby, Mary A., *An Evaluation of Alternative Channels of Distribution: An Efficiency Model.* East Lansing, MI, Michigan State University Press, 1977.

Longman, Donald R., *Distribution Cost Analysis.* Salem, NH, Ayer Co., 1978.

Robeson, James F. and Robert G. House, eds., *The Distribution Handbook.*

## DRUG USE AMONG EMPLOYEES

If you have a problem with drug users on your staff, we urge you to read the following advertisement sponsored by Partnership for a Drug-Free America:

"Drug use is a question of extremes. People who use drugs are either addicted or in danger of addiction."

"The results of drug addiction are poor performance, absenteeism, theft, robbery, industrial accidents and death."

"And addicts often take others down with them. Loved ones, co-workers even employers."

"Addicts seldom get well or even get into treatment by themselves. Someone has to help. You could be that person. If you're willing to get involved."

"When you say, in no uncertain terms, 'Get well or get out,' you may be awakening the addict to the one reality that can save her."

"Threatening to fire an addict is the worst thing you can do to her. Or the best. If it gets her into treatment."

"To find out how to set up a treatment program in your company, please call 1-800-843-4971. That's the National Institute on Drug Abuse hot line for managers and CEOs. It's manned by trained Employee Assistance Program planners and designers, from Monday through Friday, 9:00 a.m. to 8:00 p.m. Eastern Time. They won't tell you what to do, but they can outline the options."

Narcotics Anonymous is a program with a 12-step plan to aid rehabilitation wherein recovering addicts (at regularly scheduled meetings), offer help to others who seek recovery.

### For Further Information

Narcotics Anonymous
PO Box 9999
Van Nuys, CA 91409
Phone: 818-780-3951

U.S. Department of Justice
Drug Enforcement Administration
1405 1st Street, NW
Washington, DC 20537
Phone: 202-633-1000

U.S. Department of Health and Human Services
Information Center
Washington, DC 20201
Phone: 202-245-6296

## DRUG USE AMONG EMPLOYEES (continued)

Two special agencies within the Department are: Alcohol, Drug Abuse, and Mental Health Administration, Phone: 301-443-3875; and National Institute on Drug Abuse, Phone: 301-443-6847.

In many communities there are information and treatment centers for those with drug problems. Look in the yellow pages under "Drug Abuse and Addiction."

## ECONOMIC EDUCATION

Readers interested in broadening their background in economic education may be interested in the Foundation for Economic Education. It "works to improve the individual's understanding of the free market, private property, limited government way of life and its philosophical antecedents. To this end FEE has remained a consistent proponent of the ideal concept of human liberty and a critic of collectivism in its many forms. . . . We do not tell anyone how to run his life; instead we try to explain how the free market makes for social harmony and peace. We do not participate in the political process; instead we present the rationale of limited government. We take no sides on specific legislation; instead we set forth the broad principles that should underlie all law."

The Foundation's 40-page monthly study journal, *The Freeman*, is sent to anyone in the United States at his or her request. A newsletter tells of recent and forthcoming meetings, books, and other activities. An annual catalog, *A Literature of Freedom*, presenting books available from FEE and works of others as well as its own, is also obtainable upon request. The Foundation is supported by voluntary contributions and does not accept nor solicit government funding.

### For Further Information

Foundation for Economic Education
Irvington-on-Hudson, NY 10533
Phone: 914-591-7230

## EMPLOYEE LEASING

A new concept in employee relations is employee leasing whereby your employees are put on the payroll of an employee leasing company and then it leases the personnel back to you. The employees continue to work for you as before, but the company handles all the payroll paperwork, government reporting, compliance with government regulations, payroll taxes and unemployment claims.

Your staff members receive the same salary, report to the same people, do the same work, but may receive larger fringe benefits than most small businesses can afford. The leasing company can purchase fringe benefits at a much lower rate and still save you more money than if you handled these functions yourself. It is asserted that the service is available to companies with one or hundreds of employees.

### For Further Information

National Staff Leasing Association
15910 Ventura Boulevard
Encino, CA 91436
Phone: 818-986-9121

# EMPLOYMENT AGENCIES

Private employment agencies are generally listed in the yellow pages of the phone book under the heading: "Employment Agencies." It should be remembered that the state employment security office at your state capital (and possibly branch offices as well) offers similar services at no charge. It is usually customary for the employer (not the employee as was previously the case) to pay the private agency fee.

Many employers prefer to deal with private agencies because they screen applicants more carefully than the public agencies and tend to send the best qualified people. Nevertheless, it may be wise to contact the state agency in addition to private organizations. For the address and phone number of your state employment security agency see STATE EMPLOYMENT SECURITY AGENCIES.

### Suggested Reference

"Job-Hunting: Should You Pay?" Available from Federal Trade Commission, Washington, DC 20580. (Contains hints on selecting an employment service and descriptions of three major types of employment firms.)

# EXPORTING

If you plan to broaden your markets by exporting some or all of your products, you will probably need the services of a freight forwarder. International freight forwarders are licensed by the Federal Maritime Commission to provide the know-how and experience needed to move cargo from inland points to foreign destinations with efficiency and speed and at the least possible cost to the exporter.

The forwarder will advise you as to the best port of shipment, prepare and check on various shipping documents and necessary licenses, book space on an ocean vessel, arrange transportation of the cargo to shipside by truck or rail, arrange cargo insurance, pay the ocean freight and oversee all details of the shipment.

If your shipment is one which must go by air, contact the air cargo department of the nearest airline for information. You will find airlines listed in your yellow pages under "Air Cargo Service."

The National Customs Brokers & Forwarders Association of America, Inc. publishes a membership directory of freight forwarders which may be purchased from the Association. The members are listed both alphabetically and geographically. The directory also contains a Federal Maritime Commission directory which includes addresses and phone numbers of district offices.

### For Further Information

National Customs Brokers & Forwarders Association of America, Inc.
5 World Trade Center
New York, NY 10048
Phone: 212-432-0050

Federal Maritime Commission
1100 L Street, NW
Washington, DC 20573
Phone: 202-523-5911

### Suggested References

A Handbook on Financing U.S. Exports. Washington, D.C., Machinery & Allied Products Institute, 1979.

Goldsmith, Howard R., How To Make a Fortune in Import-Export. Englewood Cliffs, NJ, Reston Publishing, 1981.

## EXPORTING (continued)

ICS Group, *How to Master Export-Import Documentation.* Irvine, CA, International Commercial Service.

International Trade Books, *Official Export Guide.* Philadelphia, International Trade Books, annual, with supplements.

**Note:** This 1,500-page very complete reference book costs $220 prepaid. It is primarily a tool for freight forwarders and is not recommended for the small exporter unless he has a need for all of this information.

## FAMILY BUSINESS MANAGEMENT

Family businesses can develop unique problems which many business management consultants find difficult to solve. The consulting firm listed below specializes in this practice and three publications which may be of interest to owners of family businesses are also named.

### For Further Information

Center for Family Business
P.O. Box 24268
Cleveland, OH 44124
Phone: 216-442-0800

### Suggested References

*Managing the Family-Owned Business* (7 articles covering special problems and advantages). New York, American Management Association.

Bork, David, *Family Business Risky Business, How to Make It Work.* New York, AMACOM, 1983.

Ward, John L., *Keeping the Family Business Healthy: How to Plan for Continuing Growth, Profitability and Family Leadership.* San Francisco, Jossey-Bess, 1982.

# FEDERAL BANK LOANS FOR FARMERS AND FISHERMEN

"The Farm Credit Administration is responsible for the regulation and examination of the borrower-owned banks and associations and their service organizations that comprise the cooperative Farm Credit System. These institutions are the federal land banks that make long-term loans on farm or rural real estate, or real estate connected with a commercial fisherman's operation, through local federal and intermediate-term loan funds to production credit associations and other institutions financing farmers, ranchers, rural homeowners, owners of farm-related businesses and commercial fishermen; and the banks for cooperatives that make loans of all kinds to agricultural and aquatic cooperatives. They loan funds, provided borrowers are obtained mostly through the sale of securities to investors in the nation's capital markets." This description of the Farm Credit Administration appears in the *U.S. Government Manual* but the workings of this administration are too complicated to detail here.

If you are interested in learning more about the possibility of qualifying for a loan through this source, write to the office mentioned below for information.

### For Further Information

Congressional and Public Affairs Division
Farm Credit Administration
1501 Farm Credit Drive, McLean, VA 22102
Phone: 703-883-4056

**See also:** SMALL BUSINESS ADMINISTRATION

# FEDERAL GOVERNMENT

Determining what the federal government does and how it affects the individual or where one can find information about it is not always easy. Perhaps the best place to start your search is one of the Federal Information Centers maintained throughout the country by the General Services Administration. Persons interested in various aspects of the federal government, including its programs and services, may visit, phone, or write the Federal Information Centers listed on page 46.

### Legislative Branch

A list of Senators and Representatives is included in the *United States Government Manual* (see below). Members' offices of both houses may be reached by phone by calling 202-224-3121.

### General Information

The United States Government Manual is the official handbook of the federal government. It describes the proposals and programs of most government agencies and lists the top personnel. Briefer statements are included for the quasi-official agencies and certain international organizations.

*United States Government Manual.* Washington, DC, Superintendent of Documents, annual, 1935– .

Lesko, Matthew, *Information USA.* New York, Viking, 1986.

### Presidential Documents

The *Weekly Compilation of Presidential Documents* contains available transcripts of the President's news conferences, messages to Congress, public speeches, remarks, statements and other Presidential materials released by the White House. The *Public Papers of the Presidents* is an annual compilation of the materials contained in the weekly publication.

*Weekly Compilation of Presidential Documents.* Washington, DC, Superintendent of Documents, weekly.

*Public Papers of the Presidents.* Washington, DC, Superintendent of Documents, annual.

## Federal Information Centers—General Services Administration

| State/City | Telephone[1] | Address[2] |
|---|---|---|
| ALABAMA: | | 75 Spring St. SW., Atlanta, GA 30303 |
|   Birmingham | 205-322-8591 | |
|   Mobile | 205-438-1421 | |
| ALASKA: Anchorage | 907-271-3650 | Box 33, 701 C St., 99513 |
| ARIZONA: Phoenix | 602-261-3313 | 880 Front St., San Diego, CA 92188 |
| ARKANSAS: Little Rock | 501-378-6177 | 819 Taylor St., Fort Worth, TX 76102 |
| CALIFORNIA: | | |
|   Los Angeles | 213-894-3800 | 300 N. Los Angeles St., 90012 |
|   Sacramento | 916-551-2380 | Rm. 215, 415 Capitol Mall, 95814 |
|   San Diego | 619-293-6030 | 880 Front St., 92188 |
|   San Francisco | 415-556-6600 | Box 36082, 450 Golden Gate Ave., 94012 |
|   Santa Ana | 714-836-2386 | 880 Front St., San Diego, CA 92188 |
| COLORADO: | | P.O. Box 25006, Denver, 80225 |
|   Colorado Springs | 303-471-9491 | |
|   Denver | 303-236-7181 | |
|   Pueblo | 303-544-9523 | |
| CONNECTICUT: | | Rm. 2-110, 26 Federal Plaza, New York, NY 10278 |
|   Hartford | 203-527-2617 | |
|   New Haven | 203-624-4720 | |
| FLORIDA: | | Rm. 105, 144 1st Ave. S., St. Petersburg, 33701 |
|   Ft. Lauderdale | 305-522-8531 | |
|   Jacksonville | 904-354-4756 | |
|   Miami | 305-350-4155 | |
|   Orlando | 305-422-1800 | |
|   St. Petersburg | 813-893-3495 | |
|   Tampa | 813-229-7911 | |
|   West Palm Beach | 305-833-7566 | |
| GEORGIA: Atlanta | 404-331-6891 | 75 Spring St. SW., 30303 |
| HAWAII: Honolulu | 808-546-8620 | Box 50091, 300 Ala Moana Blvd., 96850 |
| ILLINOIS: Chicago | 312-353-4242 | 33d Floor, 230 S. Dearborn St., 60604 |
| INDIANA: | | Rm. 7411, 550 Main St., Cincinnati, OH 45202 |
|   Gary | 219-883-4110 | |
|   Indianapolis | 317-269-7373 | |
| IOWA: From all points | 800-532-1556 | 215 N. 17th St., Omaha, NE 68102 |
| KANSAS: From all points | 800-432-2934 | Rm. 2616, 1520 Market St., St. Louis, MO 63103 |
| KENTUCKY: Louisville | 502-582-6261 | Rm. 7411, 550 Main St., Cincinnati, OH 45202 |
| LOUISIANA: New Orleans | 504-589-6696 | 515 Rusk Ave., Houston, TX 77002 |
| MARYLAND: Baltimore | 301-962-4980 | Rm. 4134, 9th and Market Sts., Philadelphia, PA 19107 |
| MASSACHUSETTS: Boston | 617-223-7121 | Rm. 812, McCormack Post Office and Courthouse Bldg., 02109 |
| MICHIGAN: | | Rm. M-25, 477 Michigan Ave., Detroit, 48226 |
|   Detroit | 313-226-7016 | |
|   Grand Rapids | 616-451-2628 | |
| MINNESOTA: Minneapolis | 612-349-5333 | 33d Floor, 230 S. Dearborn St., Chicago, IL 60604 |
| MISSOURI: | | Rm. 2616, 1520 Market St., St. Louis, 63103 |
|   St. Louis | 314-425-4106 | |
|   From elsewhere in Missouri | 800-392-7711 | |
| NEBRASKA: | | 215 N. 17th St., Omaha, 68102 |
|   Omaha | 402-221-3353 | |
|   From elsewhere in Nebraska | 800-642-8383 | |
| NEW JERSEY: Northern NJ | | Rm. 2-110, 26 Federal Plaza, New York, NY 10278 |
|     Southern NJ | | Rm. 4134, 9th and Market Sts., Philadelphia, PA 19107 |
|   Newark | 201-645-3600 | |

## Federal Information Centers—General Services Administration (continued)

| State/City | Telephone[1] | Address[2] |
|---|---|---|
| Trenton | 609-396-4400 | |
| NEW MEXICO: Albuquerque | 505-766-3091 | 819 Taylor St., Fort Worth, TX 76102 |
| NEW YORK: | | |
| Albany | 518-463-4421 | |
| Buffalo | 716-846-4010 | 111 W. Huron, 14202 |
| New York | 212-264-4464 | Rm. 2-110, 26 Federal Plaza, 10278 |
| Rochester | 716-546-5075 | |
| Syracuse | 315-476-8545 | |
| NORTH CAROLINA: Charlotte | 704-376-3600 | 75 Spring St. SW., Atlanta, GA 30303 |
| OHIO: | | Rm. 7411, 550 Main St., Cincinnati, 45202 |
| Akron | 216-375-5638 | |
| Cincinnati | 513-684-2801 | |
| Cleveland | 216-522-4040 | |
| Columbus | 614-221-1014 | |
| Dayton | 513-223-7377 | |
| Toledo | 419-241-3223 | |
| OKLAHOMA: | | 819 Taylor St., Fort Worth, TX 76102 |
| Oklahoma City | 405-231-4868 | |
| Tulsa | 918-584-4193 | |
| OREGON: Portland | 503-221-2222 | Rm. 321, 1220 SW. 3d Ave., 97204 |
| PENNSYLVANIA: | | Rm. 4134, 9th and Market Sts., Philadelphia, 19107 |
| Philadelphia | 215-597-7042 | |
| Pittsburgh | 412-644-3456 | |
| RHODE ISLAND: Providence | 401-331-5565 | Rm. 812, McCormack Post Office and Courthouse Bldg., Boston, MA 02109 |
| TENNESSEE: | | 75 Spring St. SW., Atlanta, GA 30303 |
| Chattanooga | 615-265-8231 | |
| Memphis | 901-521-3285 | |
| Nashville | 615-242-5056 | |
| TEXAS: | | |
| Austin | 512-472-5494 | 515 Rusk Ave., Houston, 77002 |
| Dallas | 214-767-8585 | 819 Taylor St., Ft. Worth, 76102 |
| Fort Worth | 817-334-3624 | 819 Taylor St., 76102 |
| Houston | 713-229-2552 | 515 Rusk Ave., 77002 |
| San Antonio | 512-224-4471 | 515 Rusk Ave., Houston, 77002 |
| UTAH: Salt Lake City | 801-524-5353 | P.O. Box 25006, Denver, CO 80225 |
| VIRGINIA: | | Rm. 4134, 9th and Market Sts., Philadelphia, PA 19107 |
| Norfolk | 804-441-3101 | |
| Richmond | 804-643-4928 | |
| Roanoke | 703-982-8591 | |
| WASHINGTON: | | Rm. 321, 1220 SW. 3d Ave., Portland, OR 97204 |
| Seattle | 206-442-0570 | |
| Tacoma | 206-383-5230 | |
| WISCONSIN: Milwaukee | 414-271-2273 | 33d Floor, 230 S. Dearborn St., Chicago, IL 60604 |

[1]Call the listing closest to you for a free call or minimum long-distance charge.
[2]Some Center offices are located in other States.

## FEDERAL GOVERNMENT (continued)

### Congressional Documents

The "Slip Laws" are pamphlet prints of each public and private law enacted by Congress. They are issued a few days after becoming law and may be obtained by writing to the Public Document Room of the U.S. Senate, Washington, DC 20510, or the House of Representatives, Washington, DC 20515.

All laws enacted by Congress are contained in a volume titled the *United States Code* which was last issued in 1977 and kept up to date by annual supplements. Proceedings of Congress, speeches, debates and actions of Congress and its committees are published in the *Congressional Record* which is issued each day Congress is in session. The *Record* contains a fortnightly index and final index at the end of each session of Congress.

The *Congressional Directory,* issued annually, contains brief biographical sketches of all the members of Congress, members of the Cabinet, and the judiciary, together with their official addresses and telephone numbers; personnel of Congressional Committees, personnel and organization of the judiciary, executive boards and other commissions.

*Congressional Record.* Washington, D.C., Government Printing Office, daily, 1873– .

*Official Congressional Directory.* Washington, D.C., Government Printing Office, annual, 1809– .

*United States Code: containing the general and permanent laws of the United States in force on January 3, 1977.* Washington, D.C., Government Printing Office, annual supplements.

For further information concerning the United States Senate contact the Secretary of the Senate, The Capitol, Washington, DC 20510, telephone, 202-225-2115; Clerk of the House of Representatives, The Capitol, Washington, DC 20515, telephone, 202-225-7000.

### Federal Agency Regulations

The *Federal Register,* published daily, is the medium for making available to the public all federal agency regulations and other legal documents of the executive branch. It also carries proposed changes in regulated areas. The *Code*

## FEDERAL GOVERNMENT (continued)

*of Federal Regulations* is the annual cumulation of executive agency regulations published in the daily *Federal Register,* combined with regulations issued previously and still in effect. This serves as a convenient reference for those desiring a comprehensive source of general and permanent federal regulations.

*Code of Federal Regulations.* Washington, D.C., Government Printing Office, annual.

*Federal Register.* Washington, D.C., Government Printing Office, daily, 1936– .

### Federal Government Publications

The Government Printing Office sells through mail orders and government bookstores over 25,000 different publications which have originated in various government agencies. It also administers the depository library program through which selected government publications are made available in libraries throughout the country.

Orders and inquiries concerning publications for sale by the Government Printing Office should be directed to the Superintendent of Documents, Government Printing Office, Washington, DC 20402; telephone, 202-783-3238. A list of depository libraries is available from the Superintendent of Documents, and popular Government publications may be purchased at Government Printing Office Bookstores located in principal cities. The Printing Office also issues a monthly catalog of all publications issed by the various departments and agencies each month.

### Suggested References

*Guide to U.S. Government Serials and Periodicals.* Washington, DC, Superintendent of Documents.

*Monthly Catalogue of United States Government Publications.* Washington, DC, Superintendent of Documents, monthly, 1895– .

*Price Lists.* Washington, DC, Government Printing Office, revised frequently. (Each of these small pamphlets lists the government publications still available in the field covered. Request a list of current titles from the Superintendent of Documents, Washington, DC 20402.)

# FEDERAL TRADE COMMISSION

"The objective of the Federal Trade Commission is to maintain competitive enterprise as a keystone of the American economic system. Although the duties of the Commission are many and varied, the foundation of public policy underlying all these duties is essentially the same: to prevent the free enterprise system from being fettered by monopoly or restraints on trade or corrupted by unfair or deceptive trade practices."

"In brief, the Commission is charged with keeping competition both free and fair."

The Commission has two principal missions: (a) Consumer Protection: enforcing the Consumer Credit Protection Act, the Truth-in-Lending Act, and the Fair Credit Reporting Act; and (b) Encouraging competition: enforcing the Federal Trade Commission Act, the Clayton (anti-trust) Act, and the Robinson-Patman Act (prohibiting companies from discriminating among other companies that are its customers in terms of price or other services).

## For Further Information

Director
Office of Public Affairs
Federal Trade Commission
Washington, DC 20580
Phone: 202-523-3830

## Suggested References

" 'Best Sellers' for Business" lists Federal Trade Commission business publications available from either the Commission or the Superintendent of Documents. Send to the above address for a copy.

**See also:** CONSUMER COMPLAINTS, TRUTH-IN-LENDING LAW, USED CAR RULE

# FINANCIAL NEWS PUBLICATIONS

There are a number of periodicals and newspapers which report financial news. Since editorial policies differ widely it is wise to read one or two issues before subscribing. If the local library does not have copies of magazines of possible interest, write the publishers of those magazines which you think may prove helpful and ask the cost of purchasing a sample copy. (You may receive it gratis!) A very select list of financial publications follows, these being of very general interest.

*Barrons National Business and Financial Weekly,* 22 Cortlandt Street, New York, NY 10007.

*Financial World, The News Magazine for Investors,* 1450 Broadway, New York, NY 10018.

*Forbes,* 1271 Avenue of the Americas, New York, NY 10020.

*OTC Review,* 110 Pennsylvania Avenue, Oreland, PA 19075.

*Wall Street Journal,* 200 Burnett Road, Chicopee, MA 01020.

For a directory of newspapers and periodicals published in the United States see the *Gale Directory of Publications,* Detroit, Gale, annual. This was formerly titled *Ayers Directory.*

**See also:** INVESTMENT ADVICE

## FINANCING A BUSINESS

Banks are the best source of capital for small and medium size businesses, and it should be remembered that they are subject to both state and federal banking regulations. If Bank A turns down an application, it is possible that Bank B will approve it. Hence it may be wise to seek financing from more than one institution.

Most banks extend three types of loans: short (30, 60 or 90 days but no longer than one year); intermediate (three to five years generally), and long term (five or 10 years, usually not available for small businesses).

The Small Business Administration makes loans by guaranteeing loans made by a bank, and sometimes extending loans directly to borrowers. There is no minimum amount but the maximum sum the SBA will guarantee varies from $150,000 to $500,000 depending on the type of loan. The best course of action is to start with one's bank, and if it appears desirable to approach the SBA, then contact the nearest office.

### For Further Information

If the Small Business Administration is not listed in your phone directory under United States Government, write to:

Small Business Administration
1441 L Street, NW
Washington, DC 20416
Phone: 202-653-6365

### Suggested References

Holt, Herman, *2001 Sources of Financing for Small Business.* New York, Arco Publishing, 1983.

Ruben, Richard L., Philip Goldberg, *The Small Business Guide to Borrowing Money.* New York, McGraw-Hill, 1980.

The Small Business Administration issues two free pamphlets worth sending for: "Business Loans from the SBA," and "Your Business and the SBA." The agency also publishes a number of helpful booklets. Send for "Business Development Booklets," Form 115B (available from the Superintendent of Documents, Government Printing Office, Washington, DC 20402), and "Business Development Pamphlets," Form 115A (available from the Small Business Administration, PO Box 15434, Fort Worth, TX 76119).

## FIRE PROTECTION

The National Fire Protection Association, whose membership includes over 36,000 professionals in the fire protection field, publishes a wide range of materials on fire safety. Since its founding in 1896 the NFPA has been considered the leading authority on fire prevention and protection. Its activities are focused on two major areas: educational and technical.

Among the innumerable publications and video aids of interest to businessmen are several dealing with plant protection, fire brigade training, fire detectors, employee training and evacuation, and industrial fire hazards. All materials may be purchased by non-members. A complete catalog is available on request.

### For Further Information

National Fire Protection Association
Batterymarch Park
Quincy, MA 02269-9904
Phone: 617-770-3000

### Suggested References

*Books in Print* which may be seen at many libraries and bookstores contains a large listing of books on fire prevention and protection.

# FIRST FACTS AND WORLD RECORDS

### Suggested References

Kane, Joseph Nathan, *Famous First Facts.* New York, H. W. Wilson, 1981. A compendium of over 9,000 famous first events, happenings, discoveries, and inventions which have occurred throughout American history from 1007 to 1980. Arranged alphabetically by subject with extensive cross indexing.

*Guiness Book of World Records.* New York, Sterling Publishing, 1987.

# FITNESS IN BUSINESS

The Association for Fitness in Business has as its slogan, "Promoting Employee Health and Fitness." It accomplishes this by publishing essential data and current information, developing programs of continuing education, stimulating appropriate research, facilitating career development, encouraging professional networking, generating timely evaluations of the field, providing dynamic leadership and creating cooperative projects with other national groups. The association holds a five-day annual conference and operates through numerous regional chapters.

Membership is open to those who are not professionally employed by a company and serve as a fitness director but have an active interest in fitness, health or recreation.

### For Further Information

Association for Fitness in Business
965 Hope Street
Stamford, CT 06907
Phone: 203-359-2188

# FORMS OF BUSINESS ORGANIZATIONS

Every business establishment can be classified as one of the following:

**Single Proprietorship:** A business owned and controlled by an individual. Retail stores, service establishments and other small concerns or manufacturing firms are usually owned by single proprietors. Regardless of size, if there is one owner, the company is known as a single proprietorship.

**Partnership:** Two or more individuals who have agreed to pool their capital, work together and share the profits and the risks of conducting a business, constitute a partnership. Most partnerships are formed by brokers, lawyers, architects, doctors and other professional men and women.

**Stock Corporation:** In the United States the stock corporation is the usual style of organization adopted by both large and small business concerns.

To organize a corporation it is necessary first to obtain a charter (license) from the state. Once incorporated, shares of stock are sold at a price decided upon by those who organized the company. The money thus obtained is used to finance the new business, build or rent a factory, purchase machinery and raw materials and hire the employees. Later, when more money is needed to expand the business, additional stock may be issued and sold to the public.

The people who buy the stock are called shareholders or stockholders. They are the actual owners of the business and share in the profits of the corporation, each in proportion to the amount of stock he or she owns. It is a risk to buy stock, for should the business fail, the stockholders might lose all their money. On the other hand, if the company prospers and makes a good profit, the shareholders may reasonably expect to receive some of the profits in the form of dividends. Usually part of the profits are kept for use in the business so it can expand.

A corporation issues stock when it is originally organized or at rare intervals when it needs to raise additional funds. Many people, when they purchase stock of a company that is actively traded on a national exchange, think that their purchase is helping the company by providing additional cash. This is not true unless the com-

# FORMS OF BUSINESS ORGANIZATIONS (continued)

pany just happens at that very time to be issuing new stock. Shares of stock that are bought and sold daily by the public represent the same shares that were originally issued at the time the company was started or when additional shares were issued. The company has nothing to do with buying and selling its stock except to issue new stock certificates when asked to do so by the person who has purchased shares from another and wants the ownership changed to him.

Thus the shareholders own the company and elect the directors (or managers) of the company. They oversee the general management and are responsible for planning the business policies. They elect the officers who are responsible for the actual day to day operation of the company and who appoint the employees to serve under them.

**See also:** CORPORATION–ADVANTAGES, CORPORATE SECRETARY FUNCTIONS, INCORPORATING A BUSINESS

# FRANCHISING

Essentially there are two types of franchising: *product/trade name franchising*, and *business format franchising*. Typical of the former are auto and truck dealerships, gasoline service stations and soft drink bottlers. The franchise holder may have an exclusive right to sell the product and does so with his own marketing and selling plans and techniques. In business format franchising the franchiser establishes a fully integrated relationship with the franchise owner who provides all marketing, operating manuals and standards, and quality control. The majority of franchise companies are small, and the average rate of failure ranges from two to six percent, whereas 65 percent of all businesses fail within five years.

## For Further Information

International Franchise Association
1350 New York Avenue, NW
Washington, DC 20005
Phone: 202-628-8000

## Suggested References

*Directory of Franchising Organizations.* New York, Pilot Books, annual.

*The Franchise Handbook: A Guide to Companies Offering Franchises.* Milwaukee, DMR Publications, 1981.

*Franchise Index/Profile.* Washington, D.C., Superintendent of Documents. (SBA 045-000-00125-3) An evaluation process which may be used to investigate franchise opportunities.

Golden Square Service Ltd., editor, *The Successful Franchise: A Working Strategy.* Brookfield, VT, Gower Publishing, 1985.

Gross, Harry, and Robert S. Levy, *Franchise Investigation and Contract Negotiation.* New York, Pilot Books, 1985.

Siegel, William L., *Franchising.* (Wiley Small Business Series). New York, John Wiley & Sons, 1983.

# FRINGE BENEFITS

A fringe benefit is defined as a benefit to an employee, such as a pension, paid holiday, or health insurance, given by an employer and involving a financial cost without affecting basic wage rates.

Fringe benefits originated during World War II when government wage and price controls made it difficult to grant wage or salary increases. One way unions were able to circumvent this was to receive paid pensions instead of cash. Today the largest pension benefits are given to workers in the chemical and petroleum industries, government, public utilities and manufacturers of transportation equipment, while the lowest go to those in agriculture and construction.

Fringe benefits come in all sizes and forms. They may include a company picnic, membership in a club or Y, a recreational program, a cafeteria which serves free lunches, or hospitalization insurance, health insurance, extra holidays, use of a company car, discounts on company services or products or paid pensions.

Two facts should be remembered about fringe benefits:

1. Once employees have had them for a time they accept them as their due and no longer consider them as extras.

2. They cost money and affect profits.

Many companies make the mistake of giving expensive fringe benefits in return for a reduced wage demand, ignoring the fact that these fringes are costly and once awarded, are a fixed cost thereafter and practically impossible to withdraw.

But another angle to be considered is that most enlightened managements have generous fringe benefit programs. This makes it difficult for the small company which has not awarded these extras to its employees to entice applicants. One of the questions most job seekers ask is: "What are the fringe benefits?"

An honest answer to the effect that the company is small and struggling or cannot afford these extras but hopes to introduce some when earnings permit, is the best reply. "We put the fringe benefits into our employees' paychecks," one small business owner tells those who are curious about the company's policy.

Before adopting any costly benefit it may pay you to read one or more of the books listed below.

## FRINGE BENEFITS

**Suggested References**

Beam, Burton T. Jr., and John J. McFadden, *Employee Benefits.* Homewood, IL, Irwin, 1985.

Griffes, Ernest J., ed., *Employee Benefit Programs Management, Planning and Control.* Homewood, IL, Dow Jones-Irwin, 1983.

Meyer, Mitchell and Harland Fox, *Profile of Employee Benefits.* New York, Conference Board, 1981.

Miller, Ned A., *The Complete Guide to Employee Benefit Plans.* Rockville Center, NY, Farnsworth Publishing, 1983.

Srb, Jozetta H., Communicating with Employees About Pension and Welfare Benefits. Ithaca, NY, New York State School of Industrial Relations, 1971.

## THE FUTURE

No businessman can afford to be complacent and expect business conditions will remain unchanged. Successful corporations are always looking ahead, trying to anticipate change and plan for it. The 21st century is almost upon us and is bound to bring innovations few dream of today. Many of the signs are already visable for those who will take the time and trouble to seek them out.

**For Further Information**

World Future Society
4916 St. Elmo Avenue
Bethesda, MD 20814
Phone: 301-656-8274

Institute for the Future
2740 Sand Hill Road
Menlo Park, CA 94025
Phone: 415-854-6322

**Suggested References**

*Futurific: News Magazine of the Future.* New York, Futurific, Inc., monthly.

Karen, Ruth, editor, *Toward the Year 2000: A View from The Private Sector.* New York, Morrow, 1985.

Naisbitt, John, *Megatrends: Ten New Directions Transforming Our Lives.* New York, Warner Books, 1982.

## GRAPHIC SYMBOLS

There is a silent language we all see and recognize in street and roadside signs, at airports and terminals, and in all types of communications. The book listed below is limited to graphic symbols which give directions, instructions, and warnings—in some 26 broad subject areas.

### Suggested References

Dreyfuss, Henry, *Symbol Sourcebook: An Authoritative Guide to International Graphic Symbols*. New York, Van Nostrand Reinhold, 1983.

## HEARING CONSERVATION

It is said that over 20 million Americans are exposed to high levels of sound as part of their daily lives. Hearing loss from high decibel exposure can cause permanent, irreversible hearing loss. It is well known that many young people have or will have hearing impairments as a result of listening to the loud rock and other music to which their generation is a captive audience.

If a high noise level is a problem in your plant you may be interested in knowing that Krames Communications publishes a number of safety and health booklets and posters suitable for employee safety or health programs, including one on "Hearing Conservation: A Guide to Preventing Hearing Loss." Other booklets treat eye safety, hazards, concept of safety, respiratory protection and backs. A catalog is available on request.

### For Further Information

Krames Communications
312 90th Street
Daly City, CA 94015-1898
Phone: 415-994-8800

## HOLIDAYS

The federal government may designate holidays only for its employees and the District of Columbia; each state legislates its own holidays. Federal legal holidays are New Year's Day, Martin Luther King Day, Washington's Birthday (or Presidents' Day), Memorial Day, Independence Day, Labor Day, Columbus Day, Veteran's Day, Thanksgiving and Christmas.

The rule for the observance of holidays follows: If a holiday falls on a Saturday or Sunday, it is generally observed the preceding Friday or following Monday. A federal law passed in 1971 provides that Washington's Birthday, Memorial Day, Columbus Day, and Veteran's Day be celebrated on Monday. Government and businesses do not always observe the same holiday dates. Labor Day is always the first Monday in September; Election Day, the first Tuesday after the first Monday in November; and Thanksgiving, the fourth Thursday in November.

### For Further Information

Consult the office of the Secretary of State at your state capital for the dates when holidays will be observed in your state.

### Suggested References

*The Information Please Almanac; The World Almanac and Book of Facts.*

## HOME STUDY SCHOOLS

Home study or correspondence schools enable one to study a wide range of business subjects ranging from accident prevention, accounting, advertising, banking and finance, to marketing, merchandising, office management, weather and weather forecasting, and writing.

Home study is enrollment and study with an educational institution which provides lesson materials prepared in a sequential and logical order for students to study on their own time. Corrected assignments are returned promptly and provide a personalized student-teacher relationship.

Home study courses vary in scope, level, and length. Some require only a few weeks to complete, others call for 100 or more assignments requiring three or four years of study.

Almost 100 accredited home study schools are listed by the National Home Study Council which has served as a standard-setting agency for some 60 years for these schools.

### For Further Information

National Home Study Council
1601 Eighteenth Street, NW
Washington, DC 20009
Phone: 202-234-5100

# HOTEL/MOTEL DIRECTORY

The *Hotel and Motel Red Book* is a useful reference book for those planning a business or pleasure trip. It contains information about the following: Hotels and motels in the United States, Canada, and overseas countries; city maps; airport hotels; resorts and condominiums; travel information sources; and a "meeting planners' guide" which gives details about the facilities for meetings and conventions available in larger establishments.

## Suggested References

*Hotel and Motel Red Book*, Walnut Creek, CA, PacTel Publishing, annual.

# HOUSE ORGAN

A house organ is a publication written for and distributed among employees, sales personnel and customers. It is not easy to write a newsletter or other publication for all three audiences and make the text of interest to all groups. It is achievable, however, and *The Lamp*, published by Standard Oil of New Jersey, is an example. However, it presents, for the most part, feature articles on activities sponsored by the company or well-researched, newsworthy articles related in some way to its business.

The average small business can best publish a newsletter or publication on a regular or occasional basis which reports company activities in such a way that it interests its various readers. It takes a good writer or editor to prepare articles for two or three different readerships. Therefore, it is our suggestion that if you have half a dozen or more employees, you start with an informal newsletter and as the company expands, perhaps include major customers on your mailing list. Before sending them a newsletter, tell them that you are mailing it because you identify them with the company and appreciate their business.

A newsletter can be brief and written in a chatty informal style. It can contain news about new services or products, improvements to existing services or products, items about production innovations, thumbnail sketches of employees, suggestions for making better use of products or services and any other unusual items about the business. Employees should be encouraged to contribute and even edit on a guest basis. A newsletter can be fun to produce, help build employee morale and promote good customer relations.

## Suggested References

Arnold, Edmund C., *Editing the Organizational Publications.* Chicago, Ragan Communications.

Darrow, Ralph C., *House Journal Editing.* Danville, IL, Interstate, 1974.

Reid, Grene, *How to Write Company Newsletters.* Margate, FL, D. W. Carrey, 1980.

Travis, A. B., *The Handbook Handbook: The Complete How-to-Guide to Publishing Practice and Procedures.* New York, R. R. Bowker, 1984.

## ILLEGAL ALIENS

Under the Immigration Reform and Control Act of 1986, Congress gave legal status to aliens who had lived continuously in the United States since January 1, 1982. Effective June 1, 1987 (the deadline subsequently extended to September 1, 1987), employers could be fined from $250 to $10,000 for habitually hiring illegal aliens. If you hired workers before November 6, 1986, even though they are not eligible for legalization, you will not be subject to sanctions.

If you hire anyone you suspect may be an alien, beware! Remember that you must check everyone and obtain documentation on each employee hired since November 6, 1986, and fill out a form known as I-9 for each new worker. No business, regardless of size, is exempt from the law.

Aliens must apply to the Immigration and Naturalization Service to qualify for legal status entitling them to remain in the country. Under a more generous program certain farm workers may obtain legal status if they have worked in United States agriculture for at least 90 days during the year ending May 1, 1986. The matter of documentation and interpretation is a difficult and controversial problem. If you have questions or need to know the latest regulations, it would be wise to check directly with the Immigration and Naturalization Service.

### For Further Information

Office of Information
Immigration and Naturalization Service
425 I Street, NW
Washington, DC 20536
Phone: 202-633-4316
District offices are located in principal cities. Consult your phone book under the listing: U.S. Government.

## IMPORTING

If you plan to engage in importing, you will need a customs broker to represent you. Almost all formal entries of foreign-made goods filed each year with the U.S. Customs Service are prepared by customs brokers on behalf of their importers. Some brokers are sole proprietors, others are large corporations with branches in many ports; all are licensed and regulated by the U.S. Treasury Department. The customs broker is primarily the agent for the employing importer and often the only point of contact with the U.S. Customs Service. His duties may include advising on the technical requirements of importing, preparing and filing entry documents, obtaining bonds, depositing import duties, arranging release of goods, then delivery to the importer's warehouse or premises, consulting with the Customs Service on the proper duty rate and if necessary, pursuing remedies on behalf of his importer.

The National Customs Brokers & Forwarders Association of America, Inc. publishes a membership directory of customs brokers which may be purchased from the Association. Members are listed both alphabetically and geographically. The directory also contains a U.S. Customs directory listing the regional offices together with the principal officers of each.

### For Further Information

*National Customs Brokers & Forwarders Association of America*
5 World Trade Center
New York, NY 10048
Phone: 212-432-0050

U.S. Customs Service
1301 Constitution Avenue, NW
Washington, DC 20229
Phone: 202-566-8195

### Suggested References

Coates, Roger, *Introduction to Importing.* Dover, NH, Longwood Publishing Group, 1985.

Felber, John E., *Guide for Prospective American Importers.* Newark, NJ, Intertrade Index Printing Consultants.

ICS Group, *How To Master Export-Import Documentation.* Irvine, Calif., International Commercial Service.

# IMPORTING

International Trade Books, *U.S. Customs Guide.* Philadelphia, National Trade Books, annual, with supplements.
**Note:** This 1,500-page very complete reference book costs $220 prepaid. It is primarily a tool for customs brokers and is not recommended for the small importer unless he has a need for all of this information.

# INCORPORATING A BUSINESS

Although it is possible to incorporate your business by yourself, it may not be wise to do this without the assistance of an attorney. When you incorporate you will want to be certain that you have not overlooked any important details and your certificate of incorporation, which describes the activities your new corporation may undertake, accurately reflects your plans and expectations. It is quite possible that if you do this preparation and filing yourself, you might omit a detail which later could place unexpected restrictions on your operation. On the other hand, after consulting one or more of the books listed below, you may feel confident in your ability to prepare the papers yourself.

### Suggested References

Baranov, Alvin B., editor, *Incorporation Made Easy.* Paramount, CA, Wolcotts, Inc., 1984.
McQuowa, Judith H., *How to Profit After You Incorporate Yourself.* New York, Warner Books, 1985.
Veila C. and J. McGonagle, *Incorporating.* New York, Amacom, 1984.

## INTERVIEWING

Few businessmen are experienced or feel comfortable when interviewing applicants because they are unsure of their ability to ask pertinent questions or judge the individual fairly. Interviewing can become a time-consuming task unless one is familiar with the techniques for conducting a session and bringing it to a quick and satisfactory close. If you feel you could profit by learning from the "experts," perhaps one or more of the books listed below will prove helpful.

### Suggested References

Dobrish, Cecelia, Rick Wolff and Brian Zevnik, *Hiring the Right Person for the Right Job.* New York, Franklin Watts, 1984.

Fear, Richard A., *The Evaluation Interview,* New York, McGraw Hill, 1984.

Preston, Paul, *Employer's Guide to Hiring and Firing,* Englewood Cliffs, NJ, Prentice-Hall, 1982.

Ramsay, Roland T., *Techniques of Personnel Selection.* Chicago, Dartnell, 1980.

Sincoff, Michael Z. and Robert S. Goyer, *Interviewing.* New York, Macmillan Publishing, 1984.

## INVESTMENT ADVICE

Good investment advice can be priceless, poor advice costly or catastrophic. It is impossible for any individual to evaluate the 1,000 or more stockmarket newsletters published in the United States. However, the *Wall Street Journal* of March 27, 1987, contained an article reporting on a study by newsletter specialist, Mark Hulbert, whose *Hulbert Financial Digest* rates the performance of newsletters.

In this report Mr. Hulbert compared the 10 newsletters which he believed had the largest circulations, 20,000 to some 125,000 subscribers, and limited these to letters which emphasize picking specific stocks. Perhaps the headline best describes the gist of the article: "Rating Investment-Advice Givers: The Only Constant is Inconsistency."

### For Further Information

*Hulbert Financial Digest*
409 1st Street, SE
Washington, DC 20003

### Suggested Directory

*Oxbridge Directory of Newsletters.* New York, Oxbridge Communications, Inc.

# JUNIOR ACHIEVEMENT

The purpose of Junior Achievement is "to educate young people (boys and girls 14–21) to an understanding of the elements (capital, labor, management, production, sales and so forth) comprising the American Business System." Junior Achievement companies are established and staffed by volunteer businessmen. The Junior Achievers form a company and decide what product they will manufacture, sell stock to raise capital and follow usual business practices as they conduct their manufacturing, marketing and other business affairs.

## For Further Information

Junior Achievement
550 Summer Street
Stamford, CT 06901
Phone: 203-359-2970

# LABOR GRIEVANCES

Next to establishing a satisfactory employee compensation plan, one of the most difficult labor problems involves the handling of employee grievances. Grievances, if unresolved, can prove costly and lead to strikes and other forms of employee protests. This is why many plants have established grievance committees to deal with complaints.

## For Further Information

American Management Association
135 West 50 Street
New York, NY 10020
Phone: 212-586-8100

National Labor-Management Foundation
2000 L Street, NW
Washington, DC 20036
Phone: 202-296-8577

## Suggested References

BNA Editorial Staff, *Grievance Guide.* Washington, DC, Bureau of National Affairs, 1982.

*Grievance Arbitration: A Practical Guide.* New York, Unipub, 1977.

*How to Handle Grievances.* New York, AMACOM, 1974.

Lemmon, John A., *Family Mediation Practice.* Scottsdale, AZ, Freedom Press, 1985.

Small Business Administration, *Employee Relations and Personnel Policies.* Business Basics No. 1023, Stock No. 045-000-00196-2. Washington, DC, Superintendent of Documents.

## LABOR LAWS

If you are seeking the text of a labor law and regulations that may have been issued under it, you will find that most small or medium size libraries have little or no information about either state or federal labor legislation. Therefore, if there is no large library nearby, ask your public librarian to help you find the location of the nearest library which subscribes to one of the looseleaf services listed below.

It is possible that if the information you need is not complicated, a letter addressed to the Department of Labor* at your state capitol (for state legislation only), or to the U.S. Department of Labor** (for federal legislation) will produce the desired data. If you face a serious problem involving potential litigation or a requirement that you comply with a certain law, by all means consult an attorney.

### Suggested References

Commerce Clearing House, *Labor Law Reports.* New York, Commerce Clearing House, updated periodically.

Prentice Hall, *Labor Relations Guide.* Englewood, NJ, Prentice-Hall, updated periodically.

In many states it is possible to subscribe to a legislative reporting service which provides subscribers with daily information about the progress of all legislation while the legislature is in session. Many larger libraries subscribe to these services. For further information inquire at your public library or your state labor department.

*See STATE LABOR DEPARTMENTS for correct names, addresses, and phone numbers of all state labor departments.
**Address inquiries to Office of Information and Public Affairs, U.S. Department of Labor, Washington, DC 20210. Phone 202-523-7316.

## LABOR PUBLICATIONS

The United States Department of Labor is undoubtedly the largest publisher of books, pamphlets, periodicals, and subscription services pertaining to all aspects of labor. The breadth of coverage is suggested by the contents of the department's 1985 edition of "Publications of the Department of Labor." Here are some of the section headings: Periodicals and Subscription Services, Agricultural Labor, Apprenticeship, Collective Bargaining, Consumer Information, Employment and Training, Employment Standards, Equal Employment, Foreign Labor, Handicapped Workers, Labor-Management Relations, Mine Safety, Occupations, Prices and Living Conditions, Productivity and Technology, Public Contracts, Retirement Income Security, Safety and Health, Unemployment Insurance, Veterans, Wages, Women, Workers' Compensation and Youth.

Many state labor departments issue publications which may be more generally slanted at localized conditions or problems. Inquiries should be addressed to the Department of Labor at your state capitol (see STATE LABOR DEPARTMENTS).

### Suggested References

United States Department of Labor, *Publications of the U.S. Department of Labor.* Available from:

Office of Information and Public Affairs, U.S. Department of Labor, 200 Constitution Avenue, NW, Washington, DC 20210. Phone: 202-523-7316.

You will also want to check the current subject volume of *Books in Print* at your public library. There are almost twenty pages of books listed under the general heading of "Labor and Laboring Classes" which is broken down into many subheads.

## LEASING CARS AND TRUCKS

It is possible to save money by leasing a car or truck rather than buying one, but there are several factors to consider carefully. The booklet listed below may help you make the correct decision.

### Suggested References

*Consumer Guide to Leasing,* C.I.C., Pueblo, CO 81009. 50¢

## LEASING EQUIPMENT

Leasing enables many small businesses to acquire equipment which they could not afford because they would not qualify for long term financing. Although leasing is not always the answer, the pros and cons should be weighed carefully.

According to the American Association of Equipment Lessors, leasing "is the method most frequently used to finance equipment in the United States. Eight out of 10 American companies today use leasing to obtain some or all of their needed equipment. . . . Lessees, or users of equipment, vary widely from very small one-person operations to multi-branched Fortune 1,000 corporations. The kinds of equipment being leased are just as diverse. Transactions range from a few thousand dollars worth of equipment to multimillion dollar cogeneration facilities; from printing presses to commercial airlines; from telecommunications and office apparatus to transportation fleets." A new feature in the Tax Reform Act of 1986, the Alternative Minimum Tax (AMT), may make leasing attractive for your company.

For local leasing companies look in the Yellow Pages of your phone book under "Leasing" and "Rentals." For further information contact the association listed below.

### For Further Information

American Association of Equipment Lessors
1300 North 17th Street
Arlington, VA 22209
Phone: 703-527-8655

### Suggested References

*Consumer Guide to Leasing,* obtainable from C.I.C. Pueblo, CO 81009, 50¢.
*Equipment Leasing Is Good Business,* obtainable from the American Association of Equipment Lessors (see address above).

# LEGAL ADVICE AND RESEARCH

We do not advocate that you be your own lawyer. You can, however, inform yourself in advance about a particular situation for which you seek legal advice or representation. Knowing something about what may be involved and what the lawyer may have to do, can save time and money when you sit down to talk with him or her about your problem. In fact, you may find that what you want to do is not practical so there is no sense in consulting your attorney.

Here are the titles of a few books which may give you helpful legal background.

### Suggested References

Brown, Gordon W. and R. Robert Rosenberg, *Understanding Business and Personal Law: Performance Guide.* New York, McGraw-Hill, 1983.

Bysiewicz, Shirley R., *Monarch's Dictionary of Legal Terms.* New York, Monarch Press, 1983.

Hanna, John P., *Complete Layman's Guide to the Law.* Englewood Cliffs, NJ, Prentice-Hall, 1980.

Hempstead, Walter E., Jr., *Y.O.L. (Your Own Law) A Complete Guide for the Layman.* Houston, TX, Hempstead House, 1980.

Hermann, Philip J., *Do You Need a Lawyer?* Englewood Cliffs, NJ, Prentice-Hall, 1980.

# LIBRARY USAGE

Because most people are unfamiliar with the way libraries are organized, a few pointers may save you time and trouble the next time you seek information, a book or periodical.

### Card Catalog

The key to the book collection is the card catalog which enables you to locate a book if you know its author or title. Should you know neither and are seeking several books on a particular subject, look up that subject (subjects are typed usually in all capital letters on catalog cards) and scan all the cards to learn the titles of books which may contain information you need. Make a note of the author, title and call number of each book in the catalog that you want to examine in the stacks.

### Book Stacks

Most libraries have open stacks which means you are free to enter them and take books from the shelves to examine there or check out at the desk. If your library has closed shelves, you must fill out a "call slip" for each book you wish to see or borrow. In most libraries the books are shelved by the LC (Library of Congress) subject classification or the older Dewey Decimal System. The broad subject classifications for each are as follows:

#### Library of Congress Classification System

| | |
|---|---|
| A | General Works |
| B | Philosophy |
| C | Auxiliary Sciences |
| D | History: General |
| E,F | History: America |
| G | Geography, |
| H | Social Science |
| K | Law |
| L | Education |
| M | Music |
| N | Fine Arts |
| P | Language and Literature |
| Q | Science of History |
| R | Medicine and Old World |
| S | Agriculture |
| T | Technology Anthropology, Recreation |
| U | Military Science |
| V | Naval Science |
| Z | Bibliography, Library Science |

## LIBRARY USAGE (continued)

### Dewey Decimal Classification System

000 General Works
100 Philosophy: Esthetics
200 Religion
300 Social Sciences: Sociology
400 Linguistics
500 Pure Science
600 Applied Science
700 Arts and Recreation
800 Literature
900 History

The 600 class is broken down as follows: 610 Medical Sciences; 620 Engineering; 630 Agriculture; 640 Home Economics; 650 Business and Business Methods; 660 Chemical Technology; Industrial Chemistry; 670 Manufactures; 680 Mechanic Trades; Amateur Manuals; 690 Building Construction.

The 700 class divides as follows: 710 Landcape Architecture; 720 Architecture; 730 Sculpture; 740 Drawing; Decorative Art; 750 Painting; 760 Prints and Print Making; 770 Photography; 780 Music; 790 Recreation.

Familiarity with the broad subject letters or numbers enables one to go directly to the correct section to browse or find a particular book. Admittedly this is an oversimplification of both systems which use many numbers to break down subjects even further.

### Reference Department

Many libraries divide their reference collection into two groups: reference books shelved in the department or certain sections of the stacks, and "vertical files." Vertical files are filing cabinets where pamphlets, booklets, maps, clippings, and other ephemeral publications are stored. Contents are filed by subject and a good librarian constantly weeds out old or obsolete material to keep the file manageable. Some librarians permit the public to use these files while others do not. Almost without exception, reference books may not be taken from the building; some libraries, however, permit the borrowing of items in the vertical file.

### Newspapers and Periodicals

These are usually shelved in a special periodical room or the reference room. Only current newspapers are usually kept on open shelves. Magazines for the calendar year are generally available but previous issues may be stored in the basement or, if bound, shelved in the stacks. Space limitations may preclude the library from saving all periodicals.

### Microfilm/Microfiche

As a means of saving space, increasing numbers of libraries are buying microfilm (film on a reel or roll) copies of newspapers and periodicals which enable them to acquire many years of back issues as well as save much valuable space. Current issues are found on the shelves until the latest microfilm is received whereupon the older issues are discarded. This requires that you use a microfilm reader which permits easy searching and reading. A librarian will gladly show you how to use this.

Another space saver coming into increased usage is the microfiche card. This consists of film mounted on sheets measuring $3 \times 5$ or $4 \times 6$ inches, the size of small index cards. It is possible to reduce the page size of a book so that an entire book can be printed on a microfiche card and when inserted in a reader is easily read by the user. Although microfiche has not won wide usage, partly because it requires use of a special reading machine, it will be the answer to a library's space problems.

### On-Line Data Bases

Many larger libraries subscribe to computerized reference services whereby it is possible to see specialized reference or research data, articles, and other information on the library's terminal screen. It is unlikely that many readers of this book will need to use this type of research equipment but if your library has it, you may find it invaluable some day. There usually is an hourly charge for using the equipment.

### Searching for Magazine Articles

Current or recent periodical articles often provide invaluable information provided they can be located quickly. There are a number of useful indexes which enable one to find a specific article or several related articles on a given subject.

## LIBRARY USAGE

The following cumulative indexes, so-called because they are issued from four to 12 times a year and all the information cumulates at least into an annual volume, if not more frequently.

*Reader's Guide to Periodical Literature* indexes about 180 of the more popular magazines (approximately 6,500 are published in the United States alone!).

*Business Periodicals Index* indexes some 280 periodicals in the fields of accounting, advertising, banking, communications, computers, economics, industrial relations, international business, marketing, occupational health and safety, real estate, etc.

*Business Index* indexes books and some 350 periodicals including the *New York Times* Financial Section, but is available only on microfilm.

*Applied Science and Technology Index* indexes some 180 periodicals which specialize in subjects such as computers, energy, food industry, mathematics, mineralogy, oceanography, oil and gas, plastics, and transportation.

*Art Index* indexes some 140 periodicals which specialize in subjects such as architecture, city planning, fine arts, graphic arts, industrial design, interior design and photography.

*Public Affairs Information Service Bulletin (PAIS),* an international index, covers an enormous range of superior quality, multidisciplinary materials on business, economics, law, finance, trade and commerce, political science and much more. About 1,400 periodicals are scanned regularly for articles within the scope of PAIS. Books and reference books on subjects within the scope of PAIS are also listed selectively with reference books included comprehensively.

"All substantial bibliographies, directories, legislative handbooks, and compendia of statutes on appropriate subjects that come to the attention of the editors are listed. National and international statistical yearbooks are listed, and some state statistical yearbooks are listed. Statistical compilations for a single subject or industry are listed selectively, depending on their scope, the relative interest of the subject matter and the availability of the information in other sources. A special effort is made to list all sources of statistics of trade within and between countries.

In addition there are specialized indexes which

## LIBRARY USAGE (continued)

index various trade magazines such as *American Druggist, Consumer News, Hotel and Motel Management, Real Estate Appraisers, Interlibrary Loans* etc.

If a book or periodical which you need is not available at your library, it may be possible for the librarian to secure it through an interlibrary loan or by borrowing from the state library.

In conclusion, don't hesitate to ask a librarian for help. However, don't expect her to search an index or undertake some other time-consuming chore for you. She can lead you to the water but you have to drink. If you feel unsure when using the catalog, an index or other library tool, by all means seek assistance. This is especially true if you are researching a name, a fact or subject. The librarian is trained to seek information efficiently and should be familiar with available sources and the limitations of the library's collection.

# LICENSES

Ordinances of states and many municipalities require licenses of various types for a number of businesses. For example, a restaurant, hotel, or motel may require clearance from the local fire department, health and sanitation departments, the housing authority or building inspector, the board of alcoholic beverage control, etc. In many states licenses are required for a wide range of businesses such as automobile dealerships, electrical contracting, junk yards, lumber yards, outdoor advertising, plumbing contractors, etc.

If you are considering a business of your own, be sure to check with the municipal and state authorities before you start. If you do not know where to begin, look in the phone book for information offices listed under the city and state headings. Otherwise inquire at the city clerk's office and at the office of the Secretary of State at the state capitol.

# MAINTENANCE

Since many small businesses are operated from the home, a shop attached to the home or in a modest size building, maintenance problems are not unlike those which the homeowner faces daily. The principal difference would be maintenance of the office equipment and cars or truck which should probably be done by experts in their fields. Thus the minor repairs and other maintenance which do not call for an expert mechanic or craftsman, can be done by the owner or perhaps an employee who is knowledgeable along these lines.

There are many do-it-yourself home repair books on the market. Your library and bookstore undoubtedly have several and it would pay you to acquire one or two if you do not now own them, that is if you feel you would need guidance in making minor repairs or installations.

Some of the following books might be of interest.

**Suggested References**

Clifton, R.H., *Principles of Planned Maintenance.* Philadelphia, International Ideas, 1974.

Gladstone, Bernard, *The New York Times Complete Manual of Home Repair.* New York, Times Books, 1980.

Heintzelman, J., *Complete Handbook of Maintenance Management.* Englewood Cliffs, NJ, Prentice-Hall, 1976.

Reader's Digest, *How to Do Just About Anything.* Pleasantville, NY, Reader's Digest Association, Inc., 1986.

Schultz, Morton J., *How to Fix It.* New York, McGraw-Hill, 1978.

Sunset Editors, *Basic Home Repairs Illustrated.* Menlo Park, CA, Sunset Books, 1980.

## MANAGEMENT DEVELOPMENT

### American Management Association

The American Management Association (AMA) is the largest membership organization for professional managers who seek "a forum for personal development, sharing ideas and commitment to common goals." The more than 78,000 member managers are able to avail themselves of the following programs:

1. AMA's Center for Management Development conducts over 3,000 courses every year, covering every area of job training and career development, for every level of employee.

2. The Management Courses constitute a professional management education in four one-week sessions covering topics such as strategic planning, decision making, problem solving, team building, financial analysis, human resource management, and leadership. Attendance at all the above courses is open to members and non-members.

3. The Management Information Service gives AMA members sources of information for answers to tough management problems.

4. The AMA Library has over 100,000 up-to-date resource materials including some 12,000 books and 250 periodicals.

5. AMA publications include several periodicals, a newsletter, and a growing line of handbooks and reference materials.

6. The Extension Institute trains supervisors, managers and top executives through private, self-paced study at home or in the office under the guidance of a qualified AMA instructor.

AMA programs operate principally through its divisions, each offering a complete meeting schedule within its field. The divisions are: Finance; General Management; General and Administrative Services; Insurance and Employee Benefits; International Management; Information Systems and Technology; Manufacturing; Packaging; Human Resources; Purchasing, Transportation and Physical Distribution; and Research and Development.

There are four types of memberships: Individual, Affiliate, Corporate, and Limited Company. The last category, of special interest to small businesses, is available only to organizations with fewer than 250 employees and/or $25 million or less in annual income or budget.

## MANAGEMENT DEVELOPMENT
(continued)

### Learning International

Another company which specializes in learning programs is Learning International (formerly Xerox Learning Systems). The following quote from their brochure:

"In today's worklife, most people can't possibly work any harder. They know their jobs are competitive. They know that a lot of energy and long hours are expected from them."

"Our mission is to help those people maximize the return from all that work. But there's another side to it."

"We've found that everyone who wants to improve their productivity can do it. Cultivating that kind of positive attitude is a basic part of Learning International's mission."

"To produce training that accomplishes this isn't easy. It takes solid research, extensive testing and well-designed teaching methodologies."

"The result is training that targets critical skills to make your people more effective. Even in the face of rapid change."

The titles of a few programs and services follow: Professional Selling Skills System; Account Development Strategies; Selling Against the Competition; Telephone Prospecting; Customer Satisfaction Skills; Interpersonal Managing Skills System; Planning and Directing Performance.

### For Further Information

Membership Department
American Management Association
135 West 50 Street
New York, NY 10020
Phone: 212-586-8100

Learning International
200 First Stamford Place
Stamford, CT 06904
Phone: 203-965-8400

# MANUFACTURERS' DIRECTORIES

Frequently it is necessary to find the name of a manufacturer who makes some special product or item. The oldest and best known directory is *The Thomas Register of American Manufacturers* which consists of several volumes published each year. It can be consulted in many larger college and public libraries. It lists some 115,000 American manufacturers and in the product index you will find innumerable entries. A brand-name index is a useful feature as are the more than a thousand manufacturers' catalogs which are included.

In addition to the Thomas directory, there is Kelly's and individual state directories which can be located in *Books in Print* or the *Directory of Directories,* both found in many libraries.

### Suggested References

Ethridge, James, *Directory of Directories.* Detroit, Gale, 1983.

*Kelly's Manufacturers and Merchants Directory.* Philadelphia, International Publications Service, 1984.

*The Thomas Register of American Manufacturers.* New York, Thomas Publishing, annual. (1987 edition: 21 volumes) Available in microfilm from 1905–1977.

# MARKETING

Marketing, the exposure of products or services for sale in the marketplace, is one of the most vital functions of every business. A business stands or falls on the success of its marketing program.

The American Marketing Association accepts individuals, not companies, for membership, and invites those interested in joining to write for information. Three of the six classes of membership apply to businessmen: Associate (less than six years experience in marketing, or a baccalaureate degree and less than three years marketing experience), Professional (at least six years experience in marketing or a baccalaureate degree and at least three years experience in marketing), and Executive (all qualifications for professional membership and a minimum of ten years experience in marketing related occupations, with at least four years of managerial experience).

The Association holds numerous conferences during the year, and publishes proceedings of the conferences, as well as journals, periodicals, and books on various aspects of marketing. A copy of the "Marketing Publications Guide" is available on request; the Association publications may be purchased by non-members.

### For Further Information

American Marketing Association
250 South Wacker Drive
Chicago, IL 60606-5819
Phone: 312-648-0536

**Note:** See Gale's *Encyclopedia of Associations* for other specialized marketing associations. For books on the subject, consult the listing "Marketing" in *Books in Print,* available at most libraries and bookstores.

A marketing journal which may be of interest is the *Sales and Marketing Management,* Bill Communications, monthly.

# MEDIATION

In mediation a third party, or the mediator, recommends to the disagreeing parties various proposals or methods for settling their dispute. He imposes no solution but helps them work out their own answers. In conciliation, the conciliator merely brings the parties together and urges them to agree to any solutions which are freely offered by both sides.

The Federal Mediation and Conciliation Service helps prevent disruptions in interstate commerce caused by labor-management disputes by providing mediators to help disputing parties resolve their differences. The mediators have no law enforcement authority and rely wholly on persuasive techniques.

For disputes which do not involve interstate commerce contact the Department of Labor at your state capitol.

## For Further Information

Office of Information and Public Affairs
Federal Mediation and Conciliation Service
2100 K Street, NW
Washington, DC 20427
Phone: 202-653-5290

## Suggested Reference

Maggiolo, Walter A., *Techniques of Mediation in Labor Disputes.* Na'Alehu, Hawaii, Oceana Publications, 1971.

**See also:** ARBITRATION, CONCILIATION

# MINORITY BUSINESS DEVELOPMENT

The Minority Business Development Agency was created to assist minority business in achieving effective and equitable participation in the American free enterprise system and overcoming social and economic disadvantages that have limited their participation in the past.

Between 1968 when the program was created under Section 8(a) of the Small Business Act and 1987, more than 4,000 minority-owned businesses made use of the program which permits companies to participate for seven years. Over 700 companies have graduated from the program which is administered by the Small Business Administration.

"Management and technical assistance is provided to minority firms on request, primarily through a network of minority business development centers funded by the Agency. Specialized business assistance is available to minority firms or potential entrepreneurs.

"The Minority Business Development Agency conducts most of its activities through its six Regional Offices (Atlanta, Chicago, Dallas, New York, San Francisco, Washington) and four District Offices (Boston, Los Angeles, Miami, and Philadelphia)."

## For Further Information

Office of Public Affairs
Minority Business Development Agency
Department of Commerce
Washington, DC 20230
Phone: 202-377-1936

## Publications Available

"Minority Business Today," and "Guide to Federal Minority Enterprise and Related Assistance Programs." Order from MBDA, Information Clearinghouse, Department of Commerce, Washington, DC 20230. Phone: 202-377-2414.

## NATIONAL TELEPHONE DIRECTORY

A problem common to many businesses is locating the addresses and phone numbers of companies not located in their immediate area. Directory Assistance will give phone numbers but not addresses.

The *National Directory of Addresses and Telephone Numbers* could be the answer for many businesses. It contains a listing of phone areas and zip codes; telephone numbers and addresses for the following: business firms; government agencies; messenger, express, and postal services; air, rail and bus lines; car rental agencies; colleges; hotels and motels; hospitals; and leading American corporations. It also has a section of selected toll-free numbers.

### Suggested Reference

*National Directory of Addresses and Telephone Numbers.* New York, Concord Reference Books, annual.

**See also:** Toll-free telephone directory

## NEWSLETTERS

Almost every important area of business activity has one or more newsletters to purvey news, trends and gossip to its readership. Should you be interested in learning whether any newsletters are published for a particular business or professional field, consult one of the directories listed below.

### Directories

Domenech, Margie, Ed., *Oxbridge Directory of Newsletters.* New York, Oxbridge Communications, 1985.

Thomas, Robert C. et al, editors, *National Directory of Newsletters and Reporting Services.* Detroit, Gale Research, 1981.

# OCCUPATIONAL INFORMATION

When a businessman considers expanding his business he often needs to familiarize himself with the nature and scope of the new job positions which will be required. One good source of such information is the *Occupational Outlook Handbook* which is compiled by the Bureau of Labor Statistics and published every other year. When this book went to press in 1987 the latest issue was the 1986–1987 edition.

"The *Handbook* describes in detail about 200 occupations—comprising about three of every five jobs in the economy. Although occupations covering the full spectrum of work are included, generally those that require lengthy education or training or projected to grow rapidly are given the most attention. Thus, as the following tabulation shows, more than 90 percent of all technicians and related occupations, as well as of professional specialties, are covered, but only 10 percent of the handler, equipment cleaner, helper and laborer occupations."

| Occupational Group | Percent of Group Covered |
| --- | --- |
| Technicians and related occupations | 98 |
| Professional specialty occupations | 92 |
| Construction occupations | 90 |
| Mechanics and repairers | 87 |
| Transportation and material moving occupations | 83 |
| Management support occupations | 72 |
| Marketing and sales occupations | 66 |
| Service occupations | 63 |
| Administrative support occupations, including clerical | 53 |
| Extractive occupations | 46 |
| Agricultural, forestry, and fishing occupations | 41 |
| Production occupations | 40 |
| Managers and administrators | 13 |
| Handlers, equipment cleaners, helpers and laborers | 10 |

"Besides these 200 detailed analyses, information about 200 occupations—comprising 20 percent of all jobs in the economy—is presented in an appendix."

Another feature of the *Handbook* is the salary information which accompanies most of the job descriptions. These figures indicate the median earnings of full-time workers in 1984, and describe the earnings of the middle 50 percent of

## OCCUPATIONAL INFORMATION (continued)

workers, as well as the lowest 10 percent and the highest 10 percent. Data relates to earnings from wages and salaries only.

### For Further Information

*Occupational Outlook Handbook*
Superintendent of Documents
Government Printing Office
Washington, DC 20402

# OCCUPATIONAL SAFETY AND HEALTH ADMINISTRATION

The Occupational Safety and Health Act of 1970 covers just about every employer in the United States. The law is intended to reduce the incidence of personal injuries, illness and deaths among working men and women in the country which result from their employment. It requires every employer furnish employment to his workers, provide a workplace free from recognized hazards that are causing or likely to cause death or serious physical harm to his employees and comply with the occupational safety and health standards promulgated under the act.

The Occupational Safety and Health Administration is responsible for developing and issuing occupational safety and health standards, developing and issuing regulations, conducting investigations and inspections to see if there is compliance with safety and health standards and regulations, and issuing citations and proposed penalties for noncompliance with safety and health standards and regulations.

The Occupational Safety and Health Review Commission is charged with ruling on cases forwarded to it by the Department of Labor when disagreements arise over a safety and health inspection. Employers have the right to dispute any alleged job safety or health violation found during an OSHA inspection; or employees or their representatives may initiate a case challenging the propriety of the time OSHA has allowed for correction of a violation. Decisions of the Review Commission may be reviewed by the United States Court of Appeals.

## For Further Information

Occupational Safety and Health Administration
Department of Labor
Washington, DC 20210
Phone: 202-523-8017

Public Information Specialist
Occupational Safety and Health Review
   Commission
1825 K Street, NW
Washington, DC 20006
Phone: 202-634-7943

# OCCUPATIONAL SAFETY AND HEALTH ADMINISTRATION
(continued)

### Suggested References

The following selected publications are obtainable on request from the Occupational Safety and Health Administration: "All About OSHA," No. 2056; "Employer Rights and Responsibilities Following an OSHA Inspection," No. 3000; "General OSHA Recordkeeping Requirements," No. 3; "OSHA Handbook for Small Business," No. 2209. For a list of publications see the "Publications of the U.S. Department of Labor," (See LABOR PUBLICATIONS) or write to the Occupational Safety and Health Administration for a list of publications.

## OPTIONS FOR SELLING A COMPANY

Small entrepreneurs have different ideas about how they want to sell their businesses and what their role should be once a sale is consummated. Obviously every owner wants the highest price obtainable but realization of this goal may be affected by the timing of the payments and what the owner's role—if any—after the sale.

Options an individual faces include the following:

1. A straight cash sale called a "cashout." This is the easiest and simplest way to sell. Usually the buyer is a large corporation but once the price has been agreed upon the question is: Will the buyer want the seller to leave immediately or stay on for a year or indefinitely to continue managing the business? If a seller agrees to do this, it may mean he will demand a higher purchase price.

2. An "earn out" is another type of sale. In this situation there is a form of partnership between buyer and seller. The seller remains with the business and shares in the profits.

3. In "stock swaps" the seller receives stock instead of cash. The selling price in this type of arrangement is usually higher than in a "cash out" since the seller is probably restrained from selling the stock for a period of years, and if the value of the shares declines, he risks considerable loss on his transaction.

4. Another arrangement is part cash and part stock, probably advantageous for the buyer but not necessarily for the seller especially if he is seeking all cash.

Whatever the arrangement may be, the smart seller will consult his lawyer, tax adviser, and accountant before signing a contract of sale. Tax implications could be advantageous or disastrous, and there could be other reasons why the proposed sale could be inadvisable or the sales contract should be redrafted.

### Suggested References

Douglas, F. Gordon, *How to Profitably Sell or Buy a Company or Business.* New York, VanNostrand Reinhold, 1981.

Goldstein, Arnold S., *The Complete Guide to Buying and Selling a Business.* New York, New American Library, 1984.

## OPTIONS FOR SELLING A COMPANY (continued)

Horn, Thomas W., *The Business Valuation Manual: An Understandable, Step-by-Step Guide to Finding the Value of a Business.* Lancaster, PA, Charter Oak Press, 1985.

Miles, Raymond, *How to Price a Business.* Englewood Cliffs, NJ, Institute for Business Planning, 1982.

# PARLIAMENTARY PROCEDURE

If you are ever required to chair a meeting at which you must cope with procedural problems or even dissension, you will be grateful for the information contained in one of the books listed below. *Robert's Rules of Order* is the standard work and has been brought up to date somewhat. Some who are interested in the subject prefer the newer book written by Alice Sturgis because they feel that it copes better with the problems which arise today. Either will do and one of them should be in your public library. There are other good books on the subject too.

**Suggested References**

Robert, Henry M., *Robert's Rules of Order.* Glenview, IL, Scott, Foresman, newly revised, 1981.

Sturgis, Alice, *Sturgis Standard Code of Parliamentary Procedure.* New York, McGraw-Hill, 1966.

# PASSPORTS

It is essential to apply early if you hope to obtain a passport before making a trip abroad.

For your first passport you must present in person a completed form DSP-11, "Passport Application," at one of the passport agencies located in larger cities or at one of the thousand federal or state courts or U.S. post offices which are authorized to accept passport applications. If you have a passport and wish to renew, you may apply for a new one by mail if your last passport was issued less than 12 years ago and you were at least 16 years old when it was issued.

To obtain a passport for the first time you will need the Passport Application (DSP-11) mentioned above, proof of U.S. citizenship, proof of identity and two photographs. Passports are valid for 10 years and the fee is $35. A five year passport costs $20 and in addition there is a $7 acceptance fee charged to applicants who are required to apply in person.

For complete information about applying for passports send $1 to the Superintendent of Documents, Washington, DC 20402 and request a copy of "Your Trip Abroad"—Department of State Publication 8872—Department and Foreign Service Series 155.

Foreign governments require visas and tourist cards which must be obtained before your trip. A pamphlet, "Visa Requirements of Foreign Governments" (Department of State, Bureau of Consular Affairs Publication 9517), lists entry requirements for American citizens traveling to most foreign countries, plus where and how to apply for visas and tourists' cards. Single copies are available at no charge from the Bureau of Consular Affairs, Department of State, Washington, DC 20524 or any passport application facility.

Customs can be a problem for Americans returning from abroad unless they are familiar with the regulations. You may obtain a copy of "Know Before You Go—Customs Hints for Returning Residents" which gives you all the information you will need. Single copies are available at no charge from the U.S. Customs Service, Department of the Treasury, Washington, DC 20220. Ask for Publication 512.

## PASSPORTS (continued)

### For Further Information

Passport Services
Bureau of Consular Affairs
1425 K Street NW
Washington, DC 20524
Phone: 202-523-1355

## PATENTS

The Patent and Trademark Office examines applications for three kinds of patents: design patents (issued for 14 years), plant patents (issued for 17 years), and utility patents (issued for 17 years). Since plans and a working model must accompany the application and a patent search must be made to make certain there would be no infringement of an existing patent, it is advisable to obtain the services of an experienced patent attorney.

For a list of attorneys who specialize in patents consult your local or state bar association. See the listing for Lawyer Referral Services in the yellow pages of your phone directory.

### For Further Information

Commissioner of Patents and Trademarks
Patent and Trademark Office
Washington, DC 20231
Phone: 703-557-3341
**Note:** Operations are conducted at 2021 Jefferson Davis Highway, Arlington, Virginia.

### Suggested References

Dible, Donald, *What Everyone Should Know About Patents, Trademarks, and Copyright.* Englewood Cliffs, NJ, Reston Publishing, 1981.

Pressman, David, *The Patent Book: How to Patent Your Work in the U.S.* Berkeley, CA, Nolo Press, 1985.

The Small Business Administration publishes three New Products/Ideas/Inventions pamphlets: "Can You Make Money with Your Idea or Invention?" (MA 2.014); "Introduction to Patents" (MA 6.005); and "Proposal Preparation for Small Business Innovation Research" (SBIR–T-1). They cost 50¢ each, send check or money order to U.S. Small Business Administration, P.O. Box 30, Denver, CO 80201-0030. Allow six weeks for delivery.

# PERSONNEL ADMINISTRATION

The American Society for Personnel Administration (ASPA) is the largest national organization dedicated to the development of Human Resource Management. Through conferences, chapters, educational programs and publications, ASPA is a primary source of information on personnel policies, practices and management.

Non-members may subscribe to the society's monthly magazine, *Personnel Administrator,* and purchase any of the numerous publications issued by the society. A list, "ASPA Managing Human Resources Publications", is available on request.

**For Further Information**

American Society for Personnel Administration
606 North Washington Street
Alexandria, VA 22314
Phone: 703-548-3440

# PHOTO SOURCES

From time to time a business may require photographs for special promotional folders, publicity, catalogs or other company publications. There are innumerable sources for photographs of every conceivable subject and therefore your best course of action is to start with your local public library to see what it may have in its picture collection and what sources the reference librarian may suggest.

You will find it possible to obtain photographs free of charge from many trade associations, chambers of commerce, tourist boards, state development commissions and government agencies. In addition there are numerous "stock photo agencies" which lease or sell photographs for fees ranging upward from $10. Many of these agencies are listed in the *Literary Market Place* published annually by the R. R. Bowker Company and available in most libraries.

Actually there are so many indexes of picture sources that your library is the best place to start your search regardless of how elusive your subject may be.

# POLITICAL PARTIES

Occasionally a businessman needs to contact a politician to smooth the way to an objective or assist with a problem that has political overtones. If you are looking for the nearest office of the party in power or which can best assist you, use the phone book. Don't be surprised if you cannot find a listing. In this case call the town, city or county clerk's office for the information you need. If this is not practical ask the Secretary of State's office at your state capitol, and if all else fails, seek help from the party's national headquarters' office.

The headquarters' offices of the two major parties are given below.

### For Further Information

Democratic National Party
430 South Capitol Street, SE
Washington, DC 20003
Phone: 202-863-8000

Republican National Party
310 First Street, SE
Washington DC, 20003
Phone: 202-863-8500

# POSTAL RATES AND SERVICE

With postal rates inching up every few years faster than the cost of living index, it is imperative that businesses take advantage of every possible saving offered by the postal authorities. Accordingly, it makes good business to become familiar with the various classes of mail and rates in each to plan your mailings and shipping in the most cost effective manner possible. Many people are not aware of alternative mailing options.

For example, express mail is a bargain when compared with the charges of some private small package express firms. First class mail is expensive and it is possible to obtain the same type of service for many heavy items by using "Special Handling" which costs $1.10 for not more than 10 pounds and $1.60 above 10 pounds. Making certain that you know the difference between insured, registered, certified, and special delivery mail may save money, depending on the degree of protection and speed a shipment requires. It pays to familiarize yourself with the classifications and rates, and then see what economies you can achieve.

Because some of the rate schedules are complicated, you should talk with your postal officials to obtain complete information and assistance when reviewing your mailing procedures. The rates given below are the most commonly used and are intended for quick reference, but are by no means complete.

The following rates were in effect in the first part of 1987, subject to possible change without notice, and another general increase was expected for 1988. Pending that general increase the following rates should be in effect when this book is published in the fall of 1987.

There are four classes of mailings, each for a different type of letter or contents of a shipment.

## FIRST CLASS (includes air mail service)

| | |
|---|---|
| *1st class letters** | 22¢ first oz. |
| | 17¢ each addl. oz. |
| *Postcards* | 14¢ single |
| | 28¢ double |
| *Priority Mail* | For first class mail weighing over 12 oz. with a maximum of 70 lbs. Inquire at local post |

# POSTAL RATES AND SERVICE (continued)

*Express Mail*

office for rates from your locality.

Express mail articles received by 5:00 P.M. will be delivered by 3:00 P.M. next day. Rates include insurance, receipt and record of delivery. Rate up to 2 lbs. $10.75; over 2 lbs. to 5 lbs. $12.85; 6–70 lbs. rates vary by weight and distance. Refund given for not meeting the service promised.

* Large quantities of presorted mail qualify for reduced rate of 1¢–2¢ per postcard and 3¢–5¢ per letter, depending on level of presort.

## SECOND CLASS

Newspapers and periodicals mailed in quantity; rates vary with content, distance and level of presort. Rates for the general public when mailing occasional single pieces less than 16 oz.:

Up to 1 oz. 22¢          Over 2 to 3 oz. 56¢
Over 3 to 4 oz. 73¢      Over 4 to 6 oz. 88¢
Each addl. 2 oz. add 10¢  Over 6 to 8 oz. 98¢
Over 1 to 2 oz. 39¢

## THIRD CLASS

For single piece mailings of advertising such as booklets, catalogs or circulars; printed matter; merchandise; seeds and plants, weighing under 16 oz. Same rates as for Second Class (see above).

Bulk mailings of 200+ pieces separately addressed, rates vary according to level of presort. Bulk mailing permit and annual fees required. Consult post office for rates.

**Parcel Post** For packages of books, merchandise, printed matter, and other material not in classes of mail mentioned above, and weighing 16 oz. or more but no more than 70 lbs. Maximum size: 100″ length and girth combined. Packages over 35 lbs. and non-machinable packages subject to 90¢ surcharge. A 16¢ discount for packages

# POSTAL RATES AND SERVICE (continued)

mailed to certain local Zip areas is permitted. Consult post office for rates.

**Bound Matter** Advertising, promotional, directory or educational material weighing at least 1 lb. but not over 10 lbs. receive special rate if not eligible for Special Fourth-Class rate (see below).

**Special Fourth Class** Books, music, certain films and film catalogs, sound recordings, scripts, book manuscripts, educational reference charts or test materials, certain manuscripts and medical information for distribution to doctors, hospitals, or medical students. Up to 1 lb. 69¢; Each addl. lb. through 7 lbs. 25¢; each addl. lb. over 7 lbs. 15¢.

**Library Rates** For materials mailed to or from libraries: Up to 1 lb. 40¢; each addl. lb. through 7 lbs. 14¢; each addl. lb. over 7 lbs. 8¢.

**Note:** For Special delivery, registered, insured, and international mail rates, inquire at your post office.

## ZIP PLUS FOUR CODES

If you do volume mailings investigate the savings of addressing your list with the regular ZIP plus four numbers designating local addresses. Diskettes are available to make the conversion on computerized mailing lists.

### For Further Information

United States Postal Service, *National Five-Digit ZIP and Post Office Directory*, annual. Available from:

Address Information Center
6060 Primacy Parkway
Memphis, TN 38188-9980

This comprehensive directory may be on sale at your post office or can be obtained at the address above. See directory for current price. The directory contains complete information relating to the five-digit ZIP codes and information required by a mailer concerning U.S. Postal Service facilities and organization.

### AUTHORIZED TWO-LETTER STATE ABBREVIATIONS

| Alabama | AL | Montana | MT |
|---------|-----|----------|-----|
| Alaska | AK | Nebraska | NE |
| Arizona | AZ | Nevada | NV |

## POSTAL RATES AND SERVICE
(continued)

| | | | |
|---|---|---|---|
| Arkansas | AR | New Hampshire | NH |
| American Samoa | AS | New Jersey | NJ |
| California | CA | New Mexico | NM |
| Colorado | CO | New York | NY |
| Connecticut | CT | North Carolina | NC |
| Delaware | DE | North Dakota | ND |
| District of Columbia | DC | Northern Mariana Islands | CM |
| Federated States of Micronesia | TT | Ohio | OH |
| Florida | FL | Oklahoma | OK |
| Georgia | GA | Oregon | OR |
| Guam | GU | Palau | TT |
| Hawaii | HI | Pennsylvania | PA |
| Idaho | ID | Puerto Rico | PR |
| Illinois | IL | Rhode Island | RI |
| Indiana | IN | South Carolina | SC |
| Iowa | IA | South Dakota | SD |
| Kansas | KS | Tennessee | TN |
| Kentucky | KY | Texas | TX |
| Louisiana | LA | Utah | UT |
| Maine | ME | Vermont | VT |
| Marshall Islands | TT | Virginia | VA |
| Maryland | MD | Virgin Islands | VI |
| Massachusetts | MA | Washington | WA |
| Michigan | MI | West Virginia | WV |
| Minnesota | MN | Wisconsin | WI |
| Mississippi | MS | Wyoming | WY |
| Missouri | MO | | |

### SELECTED ABBREVIATIONS FOR STREET DESIGNATORS

| | | | |
|---|---|---|---|
| Alley | ALY | Lake | LK |
| Annex | ANX | Lakes | LKS |
| Arcade | ARC | Lane | LN |
| Avenue | AVE | Locks | LCKS |
| Beach | BCH | Mall | MALL |
| Boulevard | BLVD | Meadows | MDWS |
| Branch | BR | Mount | MT |
| Bridge | BRG | Mountain | MTN |
| Brook | BRK | Neck | NCK |
| Canyon | CYN | Park | PARK |
| Cape | CPE | Parkway | PKY |
| Causeway | CSWY | Place | PL |
| Center | CTR | Plaza | PLZ |
| Circle | CIR | Point | PT |
| Corner | COR | Port | PRT |
| Corners | CORS | Ranch | RNCH |
| Court | CT | Ridge | RDG |

## POSTAL RATES AND SERVICE
(continued)

| | | | |
|---|---|---|---|
| Courts | CTS | River | RIV |
| Crossing | XING | Road | RD |
| Dam | DM | Row | ROW |
| Drive | DR | Shore | SHR |
| Estates | EST | Shores | SHRS |
| Expressway | EXPY | Spring | SPG |
| Extension | EXT | Springs | SPGS |
| Fork | FRK | Square | SQ |
| Forks | FRKS | Station | STA |
| Freeway | FWY | Street | ST |
| Gateway | GRWY | Summit | SMT |
| Harbor | HBR | Terrace | TER |
| Heights | HTS | Turnpike | TPKE |
| Highway | HWY | Valley | VLY |
| Hill | HL | Viaduct | VIA |
| Hills | HLS | Village | VLG |
| Island | IS | Walk | WALK |
| Islands | ISS | Way | WAY |
| Junction | JCT | | |

### POSTAL COMPLAINTS

This is what the Postal Service suggests you do if you have a postal problem:

"Postal problems can usually be solved by taking them to your postmaster or customer service representative." The U.S. Postal Service also provides a Consumer Service Card Program to make it easy for individual customers to resolve their problems. Consumer Service Cards are available in post office lobbies and from your carrier and can be mailed postage free. Also, employees use them to record your complaint if you telephone the post office.

"You also have a Consumer Advocate at U.S. Postal Service Headquarters who represents the interests of the individual consumer at top management lévels in the U.S. Postal Service." If your postal problems cannot be solved locally, then write the Consumer Advocate, whose staff stands ready to serve you. The Consumer Advocate, U.S. Postal Service, Washington, DC 20260-6320.

# PRIVATE STOCK OFFERING

If you intend to raise money from family, friends, or everyday acquaintances through a private stock offering, beware! It is true that you can issue and sell stock without registering it with the Securities and Exchange Commission but the rules, permitting you to offer and sell securities even to your closest family members, may be involved. Under federal laws you may have to disclose information to the buyers, make certain that the stock is not resold to the public later and also report sales to the Securities and Exchange Commission.

State laws vary greatly but provisions of "Blue Sky" laws (see Glossary) may pertain if sales are made to out-of-state residents. It is important, therefore, that you check with an attorney before issuing any stock and making yourself liable for civil or criminal penalties as well as possibly having to return all the cash your stockholders had invested!

# PROFIT SHARING

Profit sharing can be the means of encouraging employee loyalty and dedication to the job, thus increasing productivity and earnings. The Profit Sharing Research Foundation issues a number of publications of interest to businessmen. A few of the titles appear below and a list of all the titles is available on request. The Profit Sharing Council with which the Research Foundation is affiliated, may prove helpful to you if you have questions about profit sharing.

### For Further Information

Profit Sharing Research Foundation
20 North Wacker Drive
Chicago, IL 60606
Phone: 312-868-8787

### Suggested Reference

*Profit Sharing as a Motivator, Increasing Productivity Through Profit Sharing, Does Profit Sharing Pay?* (All may be purchased from the Foundation.)

## PUBLIC RELATIONS

The practice of good public relations is as essential to the local bakery as to General Motors Corporation. Public relations is defined as dealing with people successfully, with the emphasis on an activity that is beneficial to the public or endeavors to gain the good will and understanding of the public. Publicity, on the other hand, is news that informs people about the policy laid down by the public relations program.

### For Further Information

Public Relations Society of America
845 Third Avenue
New York, NY 10022
Phone: 212-751-1940
The only professional society of PR counseling firms, practitioners, trade and professional groups, governmental, educational and other organizations in the public relations field. It sponsors local groups throughout the country and publishes an annual register of the membership and a monthly journal.

### Suggested References

Carlson, Linda, *The Publicity and Promotion Handbook: A Complete Guide for Small Business.* New York, Van Nostrand Reinhold, 1982.

Cutlip, Scott, et al, *Effective Public Relations.* Englewood Cliffs, NJ, Prentice-Hall, 1985 (6th edition).

O'Dwyer, J.R., *O'Dwyer's Directory of Public Relations Firms.* New York, J.R. O'Dwyer, annual.

Rees, David M., *Getting Publicity.* No. Pomfret, VT, David and Charles, 1984.

Two weekly newsletters are published and sample copies with subscription rates may be obtained from PR Publishing, 14 Front Street, Exeter, NH 03833, and the O'Dwyer Newsletter, 271 Madison Avenue, New York, NY 10016.

The Public Relations Society of America publishes a monthly journal: *Public Relations Journal.* Monthly.

## PURCHASING

Purchasing has attained a high state of the art in the business organization. Wise and careful buying is imperative as the quality of products and services often decline while costs increase.

### For Further Information

National Association of Purchasing Management
P.O. Box 418
Oradell, NJ 07649
Phone: 201-967-8585

### Suggested Reference

Basil, Douglas C. et al, editors, *Purchasing Information Sources.* Detroit, Gale, 1977.

*Fundamentals of Effective Purchasing.* Niles, IL, Preston.

Messner, William A., *Profitable Purchasing Management: A Guide for Small Business Owners-Managers.* New York, AMACOM, 1982.

# QUALITY CONTROL

Quality control refers to the industrial process which involves the analysis and inspection of samples of a mass produced product such as automobiles, parts, baked goods, appliances, fountain pens, etc. The purpose is to learn what should be done, if anything, in order to attain the highest possible level of quality. Inspection may be done visually or by using sophisticated X ray equipment or other testing machines.

A small business which mass produces (albeit in smaller quantities probably than a large company), must also maintain a consistently high quality level. If this is a problem in your business, you may find some of the books listed below of interest and assistance.

## Suggested References

Caplen, R.H., *A Practical Approach to Quality Control.* Brookfield, VT, Brookfield Publishing, 1983.

Crosby, Philip B., *Quality is Free: The Art of Making Quality Certain.* New York, New American Library, 1980.

Hansen, Bertrand, *Quality Control, Theory and Applications.* Englewood Cliffs, NJ, Prentice-Hall, 1963.

Montgomery, Douglas C., *Introduction to Statistical Quality Control.* New York, John Wiley & Sons.

Vaughn, Richard C., *Quality Control.* Ames, IA, Iowa State University Press, 1974.

# RADON

The latest environmental threat which is not man-made is radon, a radioactive gas that occurs in nature. You cannot smell, see or taste it, but it can threaten your health if you live in a high risk area.

Most of the publicity given radon has involved its threat to residences but it would appear that workplaces which are entirely enclosed could also be at risk. The U.S. Environmental Protection Agency conducts a Radon Measurement Proficiency Program, a voluntary program which allows laboratories and businesses to demonstrate their capabilities in measuring indoor radon. The names of firms participating in this program can be obtained from your state radiation protection office or from your EPA regional office.

## For Further Information

Office of Public Affairs
Environmental Protection Agency
Washington, DC 20460
Phone: 202-382-4361

Or write to the Public Information Office of the nearest EPA Regional Office, the addresses of which follow: Region I: John F. Kennedy Federal Bldg., Boston, MA 02203; Region II: 26 Federal Plaza, New York, NY 10278; Region III: 841 Chestnut Street, Philadelphia, PA 19107; Region IV: 345 Courtland Street, NE, Atlanta, GA 30365; Region V: 230 South Dearborn Street, Chicago, IL 60604; Region VI: 1201 Elm Street, Dallas, TX 75270; Region VII: 726 Minnesota Avenue, Kansas City, KS 66101; Region VIII: 999 18th Street, Denver, CO 80202; Region IX: 1200 6th Avenue, Seattle, WA 98101.

## REFERENCE LIBRARY FOR A SMALL BUSINESS

The office of every small business should have a basic collection of books for quick reference. It need not be large and the volumes suggested below should suffice to provide answers to most questions which may arise from time to time. These books can be purchased or ordered from almost any bookstore.

To keep informed about business and business trends, a subscription to the *Wall Street Journal* which is published Monday through Friday, except holidays, is recommended. Businessmen who want the best daily coverage of national and international news will find that the *New York Times*, published daily, is still at the top of the list.

**Suggested References**

Bureau of the Census, U.S. Department of Commerce, *Statistical Abstract of the United States.* Washington, DC, Superintendent of Documents, annual.*

Columbia University Press, *The New Columbia Encyclopedia* (one volume). New York, Columbia University Press, 1975 or latest edition.

Monroe, K.M. et al, *Secretary's Handbook.* New York, Macmillan, 1969 (9th edition) Note: If unavailable in the local bookstore, another similar volume will probably serve as well.

Office of the Federal Register, National Archives and Records Administration, *United States Government Manual.* Washington, DC, Superintendent of Documents, biannual.*

Reader's Digest, *Family Word Finder, A New Thesaurus of Synonyms and Antonyms in Dictionary Form.* Pleasantville, NY, Reader's Digest Association, Inc., 1986 or latest edition. (As an alternative, *Roget's Thesaurus in Dictionary Form,* obtainable in hard or soft cover, is recommended.)

United States Postal Service, *1986 National Five-Digit ZIP Code and Post Office Directory.* Can be purchased at many post offices or obtained by mail from Information Center, 6060 Primacy Parkway, Suite 101, Memphis, TN 38188. Note: Smaller ZIP directories are available at some bookstores and may be sufficient for the average business needs.

*Obtainable only through the Superintendent of Documents.

## REFERENCE LIBRARY FOR A SMALL BUSINESS (continued)

*Webster's New Collegiate Dictionary.* Springfield, MA, G. & C. Merriam Company, 1981 or latest edition.

*World Almanac and Book of Facts.* New York, Pharos Books, annual.

# RESEARCH

There is nothing difficult or mysterious about undertaking a research project. Research is searching out information in an organized manner and putting the data together in a logical arrangement. How thoroughly you need investigate depends on the scope of the project and depth of searching required. It can be fun to research, especially if you have an inquiring mind and are eager to find the necessary data.

One research project may recommend a solution to a problem, another may compile facts required for an important study. There is no cut and dried method for doing research, however, there are books which will help you organize your thinking and plan of attack. Thus you will save time and also come up with better results. We believe that the Horowitz book listed below is one of the best introductions and guides for undertaking research.

**Suggested References**

Golen, Steven P., et al., *Report Writing for Business and Industry.* New York, John Wiley and Sons.

Horowitz, Lois, *Knowing Where to Look: The Ultimate Guide to Research.* Cincinnati, Writer's Digest Books, 1984.

Lesikar, Raymond V., *How to Write a Report Your Boss Will Read and Remember.* Homewood, IL, Dow Jones-Irwin.

Mascolini, Marcia and Caryl Freeman, *Objective Writing for Business and Industry.* Englewood Cliffs, NJ, Reston Publishing, 1983.

Meyer, Ruth et al, *The Research and Report Handbook for Business, Industry and Government.* New York, John Wiley and Sons, 1981.

Pokress, E., *Research and Technical Writing.* Allenhurst, NJ, Aurea Publishing.

# RIGHT-TO-KNOW LAWS

A new wave of state labor law activism developed after employment regulation had evolved initially and entirely from federal legislation and regulation. Thus, although you may not be engaged in interstate commerce (therefore not subject to federal laws), you may be covered by state legislation.

One important right-to-know concern involves an employee's right to review, copy, or rebut the contents of his or her personnel file. Failure to grant access may result in a stiff civil penalty.

Another right-to-know concern is what may happen to the employee who is exposed to hazardous materials or substances present or passing through the workplace. In areas where such laws have passed, usually the employee has an "inherent" right to know about all dangers. Data sheets must be posted identifying the chemicals or other substances and giving information about the health effects, symptoms from overexposure and precautions which should be taken. Training programs for new employees may also be mandated and such regulations pertain to all companies, regardless of size.

"Whistle blowers" who report violations to the authorities are generally protected under such legislation.

If you are uncertain about the status of possible right-to-know legislation in your state, check with your Department of Labor at the state capitol. For the address and phone, see STATE LABOR DEPARTMENTS.

## SAFETY

The National Safety Council is the world's largest organization devoted solely to educating and influencing society to adopt safety and health policies, practices, and procedures to prevent losses arising from accidents and adverse occupational or environmental exposures. The Council claims that membership can have a direct impact on a company's productivity and profits because studies have shown that employees working in member organizations in industry have a 70 percent lower accident-frequency rate than employees of a nonmember company.

Membership entitles you to a 25 percent discount on all Council services. It also enables one to secure technical assistance from more than 300 professional members of the support staff who assist in developing safety and health materials and services, creating custom programs through consulting services, facilitating product development, and providing other technical assistance. Among the many benefits are a small business manual to help small business owners/managers achieve compliance with OSHA guidelines (see below), subscriptions to *National Safety and Health News* and a newsletter, various other printed materials and reduced registration rates for the annual National Safety Council Congress and Exposition, and other local and national meetings, workshops, seminars, Safety Training Institute and Driver Improvement Programs.

**For Further Information**

National Safety Council
444 North Michigan Avenue
Chicago, IL 60611
Phone: 800-621-7619 (outside Illinois)
or 312-527-4800 (in Illinois)
*General Materials Catalog:* This catalog of materials offered for sale by the National Safety Council seemingly covers every aspect of safety and is available on request.

On the subject of safety, every employer should be familiar with the provisions of the Occupational Safety and Health Administration.

**See also:** OCCUPATIONAL SAFETY AND HEALTH ADMINISTRATION.

## SCORE

Retired business executives serve under SCORE (Service Corps of Retired Executives), an organization sponsored by the Small Business Administration. These men and women volunteer their services to small businesses which seek managerial assistance. SCORE volunteers work in each Small Business Administration district office; their services are free.

**For Further Information**

If neither SCORE nor the Small Business Administration is listed in your phone directory under United States Government, write to: the Small Business Administration, 1441 L. Street, NW, Washington, DC 20416 for the address of the nearest office. Phone: 202-653-6365

# SECRETARIAL HANDBOOK

The extent and thoroughness of secretarial training varies greatly from high school vocational classes to expensive finishing-type secretarial schools. Many small businesses are unable to attract or afford the most proficient secretaries and must endeavor to help less accomplished employees attain a level of efficiency needed for the business. It is a sad fact that many high school graduates do not know the alphabet and therefore cannot file; cannot spell and therefore type letters full of misspelled words; and do not know proper punctuation, thereby running the risk of changing the meaning of sentences.

In addition to having a handbook for ready reference, a secretary should have access to (and be encouraged to use!) a good dictionary like *Webster's New Collegiate Dictionary,* a thesaurus like Roget's, and a ZIP code directory if correspondence warrants it.

Secretarial handbooks cannot retrain people but they can help make up for or correct some of the deficiencies. One of the best known is Monroe's *Secretary's Handbook* but others are listed below. Your bookstore may have one or two others equally worth considering.

**Suggested References**

Becker, Esther R. and Evelyn Anders, *The Successful Secretary's Handbook.* New York, Harper & Row, 1971.

DeVries, Mary A., *A Secretary's Almanac and Fact Book.* Englewood Cliffs, NJ, Prentice-Hall, 1985.

——*Complete Secretary's Handbook.* Englewood Cliffs, N.J., Prentice-Hall, 1982.

Lindsell, Sheryl L., *The Secretary's Quick Reference Manual.* New York, Arco Publishing, 1983.

Monroe, K.M. et al, *Secretary's Handbook.* New York, Macmillan, 1969 (9th edition).

# SELF-EMPLOYED ORGANIZATIONS

Female business owners have their own association, The National Association of Women Business Owners, which was founded in 1974. Nationally, over the last decade women have gone into entrepreneurship at a rate three times faster than men. Women own a quarter of the small businesses in the country many of whom are a major source of new job creation and innovation.

"NAWBO provides women entrepreneurs management and technical assistance, for support and encouragement of exciting new management techniques as they develop and implement business strategies, for local and national business contacts, for leadership training, for visibility, for appointments, and for increased business prosperity. NAWBO works in partnership with major corporations on programs and issues of mutual benefit and to ensure prime contracting opportunities for women business owners."

Annual dues are $75 with a registration fee of $25 and local chapter dues range from $40 to $90.

Men and women make up the 100,000 members of the National Association for the Self-Employed, a non-profit organization. "United we have clout . . . together we can sponsor group health insurance programs, negotiate money saving discounts on a wide variety of products and services, and have a voice in government. We can also share ideas, encourage and motivate one another. We can do many beneficial things together that we couldn't possibly accomplish alone. Together we can make a difference."

Dues are $42 a year with no registration fee.

Another organization of interest to small and medium sized businesses is the National Federation of Independent Business (NFIB) which represents over half a million business and professional people. Quoting from its literature:

"NIFB is a non-profit business and professional organization designed to promote the economic, financial and non-partisan political welfare of its members. It is funded solely from member dues. Each member decides how much to contribute. An upper limit of $1,000 prevents any single business from dominating NFIB policy. All small-business owners are welcome in NFIB, and all have equal say about the issues, regardless of the amount of dues they pay. An NFIB field representative can give you more details."

## SELF–EMPLOYED ORGANIZATIONS (continued)

"NFIB tells policy-makers where small-business people like you stand on the issues."

"Consider membership in NFIB because as good as legislators are, none can foresee all the effects their policymaking will have. As an NFIB member, you're not alone in speaking up. Voicing your opinion in the United States Congress and 50 state legislatures is 500,000 times more effective with NFIB."

### For Further Information

National Association of Women Business Owners
600 South Federal Street
Chicago, IL 60605
Phone: 312-346-2330

National Association for the Self-Employed
2324 Gravel Road
Fort Worth, TX 76118
Phone: 1-800-433-8004

National Federation of Independent Business
150 West 20th Avenue
San Mateo, CA 94403
Phone: 415-341-7441

## SHOPLIFTING

Most retailers suffer losses from shoplifting and many businesses are subjected also to employee theft. Some of the following books and pamphlets may prove helpful if you have shoplifting problems and dishonest employees.

### Suggested References

*Apprehending and Persecuting Shoplifters and Dishonest Employees.* New York, National Retail Merchants.

Baumer, Terry L. and Dennis P. Rosenbaum, *Combatting Retail Theft: Programs and Strategies.* Stoneham, MA, Butterworth's, 1984.

Farrell, Kathleen L. and John A. Ferrara, *Shoplifting: The Antishoplifting Guidebook.* New York, Praeger Publishers, 1985.

Francis, Dorothy B., *Shoplifting: The Crime Everybody Pays For.* New York, Lodestar Books, 1980.

Sklar, Stanley L., *Shoplifting: What You Need to Know About the Law.* New York, Fairchild Books, 1981.

The following pamphlets are available from the U.S. Small Business Administration, P.O. Box 30, Denver, CO 80201-0030, at 50¢ each: "Preventing Employee Pilferage," Business Development Pamphlet: MA 5.005; and "Reducing Shoplifting Losses," Business Development Pamphlet: MA 3.006.

# SMALL BUSINESS ADMINISTRATION

The following excerpts from the booklet entitled: "Your Business and the SBA" published by the Small Business Administration gives the principal objectives and functions of that federal agency:

"The U.S. Small Business Administration is a small, independent federal agency, created by Congress in 1953 to assist, counsel and champion the millions of American small businesses which are the backbone of this country's competitive free-enterprise economy."

"The mission of SBA, simply put, is to help people get into business and to stay in business. To do this, SBA acts as an advocate for small business; at the direction of Congress, the Agency espouses the cause of small business, explains small business's role and contributions to our society and economy, and advocates programs and policies that will help small business. SBA performs this advocacy role in close coordination with other federal agencies, with Congress, and with financial, educational, professional and trade institutions and associations."

"The Agency also provides prospective, new, and established persons in the small business community with financial assistance, management counseling, and training. SBA also helps get and direct government procurement contracts for small firms."

"The Agency makes special efforts to assist women, minorities, the handicapped and veterans to get into business, and stay in business, because such persons long have faced unusual difficulties in the private marketplace."

"The Agency has about 3,700 permanent employees and more than 100 offices in all parts of the nation. To provide quick service, SBA has delegated decision making authority to its field offices in most of the program areas. . . ."

This booklet, obtainable on request from the Small Business Administration details its programs and contains a list of all the local field offices together with their telephone numbers.

## For Further Information

Small Business Administration
Office of Public Communications
1441 L Street, NW
Washington, DC 20416
Phone: 202-653-6832

# SMALL BUSINESS ADMINISTRATION (continued)

### Suggested References

The following pamphlets are available by writing to the SBA at the above address: "Help for Small Business," "Business Loans from the SBA," "Business Development Pamphlets," "Business Development Booklets," and "Small Business Tax Workshops."

**See also:** FINANCING A BUSINESS, SCORE

## SMALL BUSINESS SERVICES

Dun & Bradstreet, Inc. traces its roots back to 1841 when Lewis Tappan, a successful New York merchant, started the Mercantile Agency to provide business information to customers who needed reliable credit reporting. In 1859 Tappan's agency became known as R.G. Dun & Company. Meanwhile, 10 years earlier, a rival, John M. Bradstreet Company was founded in Cincinnati but it was not until 1933 that the two companies merged to form the R.G. Dun-Bradstreet Corporation (renamed Dun & Bradstreet, Inc., in 1939) to provide credit information and debt collection services to business. In no time the company's name became synonymous with credit reports frequently referred to as "Dun Reports."

Since that time the company has expanded. "D&B's customers were rapidly acquiring an appetite not only for commercial credit information," the company has stated, "but for data that guided all kinds of business decisions." Some of these Dun & Bradstreet services of interest to small businesses include:

**Credit Services:** Credit reports and business and financial information services are provided, based on data collected from more than 7 million businesses in the United States.

**Plan Services:** D&B is the largest administrator of group insurance designed specifically for small businesses.

**Commercial Collection:** D&B provides debt management (1) contacting delinquent firms to produce quick and economical collections, and (2) developing more effective internal management of receivables.

**Business Education Services:** D&B offers seminars and correspondence courses to help people in credit, financial analysis, management, customer relations, sales, prospecting, planning information systems, marketing strategy, secretarial or human resources administration.

**Technical Publishing:** D&B publishes 22 business and professional magazines. One periodical of special interest to small businesses is the *D&B Reports, The Dun & Bradstreet Magazine for Small Business Management*. Some titles of articles which appeared in a recent issue give an idea of the type of coverage: "Cost management—the key to survival," "New idea, part-time con-

## SMALL BUSINESS SERVICES (continued)

troller", "Cost accounting: shows what's really profitable—and what's not", "Direct marketing", "Sorting out the health-insurance options."

For a comprehensive overview of the company's varied and numerous services, send for a copy of "This Is Dun & Bradstreet."

### For Further Information

Dun & Bradstreet
299 Park Avenue
New York, NY 10171
Phone: 212-593-6800

## SMALL BUSINESS VOICE

"National Small Business United has been looking out for small businesses' best interests since 1937. In the half century it has been in operation, the association has initiated and helped engineer the enactment of innumerable pieces of favorable federal legislation for small business."

The NSBU relies on small business owners rather than a paid staff to direct its lobbying efforts. One of the organization's goals is to help form state organizations to give small business access to state as well as federal legislative bodies. If interested in obtaining more information contact the national association at the address or phone listed below.

### For Further Information

National Small Business United
1155 15th Street, NW
Washington, DC 20005
Phone: 202-293-8830

## SMALL PACKAGE EXPEDITED DELIVERY SERVICE

Correspondence, documents and small packages which require expedited delivery, especially overnight to distant cities, may be shipped by one of the following services. Depending on the destination and ability of the carrier, one day service or overnight delivery may be guaranteed. Costs are based on weight and service rendered. All of the carriers are reliable and if contacted by phone, representatives of each will explain the types of service available.

For Express Mail Service offered by the postal service, consult your local post office. For pick up and delivery service offered by Federal Express, Purolator Courier or United Parcel, consult the white pages of the telephone directory for the 800 number of each, or the yellow pages under "Air Cargo Service". Some airlines also offer small package expedited service. Their 800 numbers also are listed in the white or yellow pages.

# SMOKING

The Bureau of National Affairs, Inc. found in a 1986 survey that 36 percent of all employers contacted had restrictive smoking policies and another 22 percent were considering them. A survey conducted in April 1987 by the Wall Street Journal/NBC News showed that tolerance toward smokers is disappearing. Over half the non-smokers were bothered by smoking and two-thirds were giving more thought to their rights than they did five years earlier.

Segregating smokers into separate areas or offices may be inadvisable because it could create a "back of the bus mentality." There is no doubt that many managements frown on smoking and believe the health hazards to smokers and non-smokers, or "passive smokers", justify a non-smoking ban. As the book went to press there were no known court cases or legal precedents for handling the problem of a workplace smoking ban.

The Smoking Policy Institute helps businesses establish smoking restrictions and may be of assistance to you.

# SOCIAL SECURITY

Many people are unaware of the fact that social security is more than an old age assistance program. It also embraces an unemployment compensation program, makes federal grants for child welfare services, public health services and vocational rehabilitation. There are cases where employees who have not reached retirement age require some of these other services.

Monthly payments of disability insurance are made to those with severe physical or mental impairments which prevent them from working for at least one year, or are expected to result in death. Payments start with the sixth full month of disability and may continue for as long as the person remains disabled. Payments may be made to the surviving dependents of an insured worker. Unmarried children can receive benefits if a worker is receiving retirement or disability checks or dies.

The federal government shares with the states the cost of basic rehabilitation programs. These are designed for people who have birth defects or have suffered an accident or illness not covered by workmen's compensation.

Under the supplemental security income program (SSI), cash payments are made to the aged, blind and disabled whose financial need makes them eligible for such additional income.

**For Further Information**

Call or write the nearest Social Security Office. It is listed in the phone directory under United States Government.

**Suggested References**

Commerce Clearing House, Inc., *Social Security Explained, Nineteen Eighty-Five.* New York, Commerce Clearing House, 1985.

Jehle, Faustin, F., *Complete and Easy Guide to Social Security and Medicare.* Guilford, CT, Fraser Publishing, 1986.

## STATE EMPLOYMENT SECURITY AGENCIES

Most state employment security agencies have two principal responsibilities: acting as a state-wide employment agency, and administering the state's unemployment compensation program.

The nation's 2,500 Job Service offices, also called the public employment service and located throughout the 50 states and District of Columbia, are run by the state employment security agencies under the direction of the U.S. Department of Labor's Employment Service. Providing help without charge, the Job Service centers offer testing and counseling services, help job seekers find employment and assist employers in locating qualified workers. All state employment security agencies develop detailed labor market data needed by employment and training specialists and guidance counselors who plan for the local needs. The matter of equal job opportunity may also fall within the responsibility of the Job Service.

With millions of Americans out of work, the unemployment security agencies assume increasingly heavy administrative workloads and financial burdens. Working closely with the Job Service offices, every attempt is made, within the scope of job availability, to find employment for those who file unemployment benefit claims.

The state employment security agency can often provide applicants for job openings (see EMPLOYMENT AGENCIES). When it is necessary to discharge or lay off employees, it is the agency to which these individuals should be referred.

#### Alabama
Department of Industrial Relations
649 Monroe Street
Montgomery 36130
(205) 261-5420

#### Alaska
Employment Security Division
4th and Harris Streets
P.O. Box 1149
Juneau 99811
(907) 465-2712

#### Arizona
Department of Economic Security
1717 West Jefferson
Phoenix, AZ 85007
(602) 255-4791

## STATE EMPLOYMENT SECURITY AGENCIES (continued)

#### Arkansas
Employment Security Division
Department of Labor
P.O. Box 2981
Little Rock, AR 72203
(501) 375-8442

#### California
Employment Development Department
800 Capitol Mall
Sacramento, CA 95814
(916) 445-8008

#### Colorado
Division of Employment and Training
Department of Labor and Employment
251 East 12th Avenue
Denver, CO 80203
(303) 844-4477

#### Connecticut
Employment Security Division
Connecticut Labor Department
200 Folly Brook Boulevard
Wethersfield, CT 06109
(203) 566-4384

#### Delaware
Department of Labor
820 North French Street
Wilmington, DE 19809
(302) 571-2710

#### District of Columbia
The Department of Employment Services
500 C Street, NW
Washington, DC 20001
(202) 631-1615

#### Florida
Department of Labor and Employment Security
Caldwell Building
Tallahassee, FL 32304
(904) 488-4398

#### Georgia
Employment Security Agency
State Labor Building
Atlanta, GA 30334
(404) 656-3000

#### Hawaii
Department of Labor and Industrial Relations
830 Punchbowl Street
Honolulu, HI 96813
(808) 548-3150

## STATE EMPLOYMENT SECURITY AGENCIES (continued)

**Idaho**
Department of Employment
317 Main Street
Boise, ID 83735
(208) 334-2731

**Illinois**
Bureau of Employment Security
910 South Michigan Avenue
Chicago, IL 60605
(312) 793-5280

**Indiana**
Employment Security Division
10 North Senate Avenue
Indianapolis, IN 46204
(317) 232-7722

**Iowa**
Iowa Department of Job Service
1000 East Grand Avenue
Des Moines, IA 50319
(515) 281-8474

**Kansas**
Division of Employment
401 Topeka Avenue
Topeka, KS 66603
(913) 296-5000

**Kentucky**
Department for Human Resources
Bureau for Manpower Services
275 East Main Street
Frankfort, KY 40621
(502) 586-5251

**Louisiana**
Department of Employment Security
1001 North 23rd Street
Baton Rouge, LA 70804
(504) 342-3111

**Maine**
Employment Security Commission
20 Union Street
Augusta, ME 04330
(207) 289-5770

**Maryland**
Employment Security Administration
1100 North Eutaw Street
Baltimore, MD 21201
(301) 383-5971

## STATE EMPLOYMENT SECURITY AGENCIES (continued)

**Massachusetts**
Division of Employment Security
Charles F. Hurley ES Building
Boston, MA 02114
(617) 727-6360

**Michigan**
Michigan Employment Security Commission
7310 Woodward Avenue
Detroit, MI 48202
(313) 876-5000

**Minnesota**
Department of Employment Security
390 North Robert Street
St. Paul, MN 55101
(612) 296-6107

**Mississippi**
Employment Commission
1520 West Capital Street
Jackson, MS 39205
(601) 354-8711

**Missouri**
Division of Employment Security
421 East Dunklin Street
Jefferson City, MO 65101
(314) 751-3215

**Montana**
Employment Security Division
Lockey and Roberts
Helena, MT 59601
(406) 444-4500

**Nebraska**
Division of Employment
550 South 16th Street
Lincoln, NE 68509
(402) 475-8451

**Nevada**
Employment Security Department
500 East 3rd Street
Carson City, NV 89713
(702) 885-4650

**New Hampshire**
Department of Employment Security
32 South Main Street
Concord, NH 03301
(603) 224-3311

## STATE EMPLOYMENT SECURITY AGENCIES (continued)

**New Jersey**
Division of Employment Services
John Fitch Plaza
Trenton, NJ 08625
(609) 292-2323

**New Mexico**
Employment Security Commission
401 Broadway, NE
Albuquerque, NM 87103
(505) 841-8408

**New York**
Department of Labor
State Campus, Building 112
Albany, NY 12240
(518) 474-2741

**North Carolina**
Employment Security Commission
200 West Jones Street
Raleigh, NC 27611
(919) 733-3098

**North Dakota**
Job Service
1000 East Divide Avenue
Bismarck, ND 58505
(701) 224-2836

**Ohio**
Bureau of Employment Services
145 South Front Street
Columbus, OH 43216
(614) 466-3817

**Oklahoma**
Employment Security Commission
Will Rogers Memorial Office Building
Oklahoma City, OK 73105
(405) 557-7100

**Oregon**
Employment Division
875 Union Street
Salem, OR 97311
(503) 378-4846

**Pennsylvania**
Office of Employment Security
Labor and Industry Building
Harrisburg, PA 17121
(717) 787-5279

## STATE EMPLOYMENT SECURITY AGENCIES (continued)

**Rhode Island**
Department of Employment Security
24 Mason Street
Providence, RI 02903
(401) 277-3600

**South Carolina**
Employment Security Commission
1550 Gladsden Street
Columbia, SC 29202
(803) 737-2400

**South Dakota**
Department of Labor
Kneip Building
Pierre, SD 57501
(605) 973-3101

**Tennessee**
Department of Employment Security
Cordell Hull Building
Nashville, TN 37219
(615) 741-2131

**Texas**
Employment Commission
TEC Building
15th and Congress Avenue
Austin, TX 78778
(512) 463-2222

**Utah**
Department of Employment Security
174 Social Hall Avenue
Salt Lake City, UT 84147
(801) 533-2400

**Vermont**
Department of Employment Security
5 Green Mountain Drive
Montpelier, VT 05602
(802) 229-0311

**Virginia**
Employment Commission
703 East Main Street
Richmond, VA 23211
(804) 786-7097

**Washington**
Employment Security Department
212 Maple Park
Olympia, WA 98504
(206) 753-5243

## STATE EMPLOYMENT SECURITY AGENCIES (continued)

**West Virginia**
Department of Employment Security
112 California Avenue
Charleston, WV 25305
(304) 348-2630

**Wisconsin**
Job Service Division
201 East Washington Avenue
Madison, WI 53707
(608) 266-1492

**Wyoming**
Employment Security Commission
ESC Building
Center and Midwest Street
Casper, WY 82601
(307) 234-4591

## STATE LABOR DEPARTMENTS

There is no organizational uniformity among the labor departments established in the 50 states and the District of Columbia. In general, these departments may be responsible for all or some of the following functions: administration of apprenticeship programs, conducting conciliation and arbitration services, enforcement of child labor laws, industrial safety inspection and enforcement, planning and carrying out various labor relations programs, enforcement of minimum wage laws, compilation and publication of labor statistics and administration of workmen's compensation programs.

For information about a state labor department, write or call the department, using the address or telephone number listed below.

**Alabama**
Department of Labor
600 Administration Building
Montgomery, AL 36130
(205) 832-6270

**Alaska**
Department of Labor
PO Box 1149
Juneau, AK 99811
(907) 465-2700

**Arizona**
Department of Labor
Industrial Commission
1601 West Jefferson Street
Phoenix, AZ 85007
(602) 255-4515

**Arkansas**
Department of Labor
1022 High Street
Little Rock, AR 72202
(501) 375-8442

**California**
Department of Labor
2422 Arden Way
Sacramento, CA 95825
(916) 920-6116

**Colorado**
Department of Labor and Employment
251 East 12th Avenue
Denver, CO 80203
(303) 866-6579

## STATE LABOR DEPARTMENTS
(continued)

**Connecticut**
Department of Labor
200 Folly Brook Boulevard
Wethersfield, CT 06109
(203) 566-5100

**Delaware**
Department of Labor
820 North French Street
Wilmington, DE 19801
(302) 571-2710

**District of Columbia**
Department of Employment Services
500 C Street, NW
Washington, DC 20001
(202) 639-2000

**Florida**
Department of Labor and Employment Security
Berkeley Building
Tallahassee, FL 32301
(904) 488-4398

**Georgia**
Department of Labor
254 Washington Stret, SW
Atlanta, GA 30303
(404) 656-3000

**Hawaii**
Department of Labor and Industrial Relations
825 Mililani Street
Honolulu, HI 96813
(808) 548-6465

**Idaho**
Department of Labor and Industry Service
317 Main Street
Boise, ID 93702
(208) 334-2327

**Illinois**
Department of Labor
100 North First Street
Springfield, IL 62702
(217) 782-6206

**Indiana**
Division of Labor
State Office Building
Indianapolis, IN 46204
(317) 232-2663

## STATE LABOR DEPARTMENTS
(continued)

**Iowa**
Bureau of Labor
307 East 7th Street
Des Moines, IA 50309
(515) 281-3606

**Kansas**
Department of Human Resources
401 Topeka Avenue
Topeka, KS 66603
(913) 295-5000

**Kentucky**
Department of Labor
Capital Plaza Tower
Frankfort, KY 40601
(502) 564-3070

**Louisiana**
Department of Labor
PO Box 44063
Baton Rouge, LA 70804
(504) 342-3011

**Maine**
Department of Labor
20 Union Street
Augusta, ME 04333
(207) 289-3788

**Maryland**
Division of Labor and Industry
1 South Calvert Street
Baltimore, MD 21202
(301) 659-4180

**Massachusetts**
Department of Labor and Industries
100 Cambridge Street
Boston, MA 02129
(617) 727-3454

**Michigan**
Department of Labor
Leonard Plaza
Lansing, MI 48933
(517) 373-9435

**Minnesota**
Department of Labor and Industry
444 Lafayette Road
St. Paul, MN 55101
(612) 296-6107

## STATE LABOR DEPARTMENTS
(continued)

**Mississippi**
Employment Security Commission
PO Box 1599
Jackson, MS 39215
(601) 354-8711

**Missouri**
Department of Labor and Industrial Relations
421 East Dunklin Street
Jefferson City, MO 65101
(314) 751-4091

**Montana**
Department of Labor and Industry
Labor and Industry Building
Helena MT 59620
(406) 444-3661

**Nebraska**
Department of Labor
550 South 16th
Lincoln, NE 68508
(402) 475-8451

**Nevada**
Department of Labor
505 East King Street
Carson City, NV 89701
(702) 885-4850

**New Hampshire**
Department of Labor
1 Pillsbury Street
Concord, NH 03301
(603) 271-3176

**New Jersey**
Department of Labor
John Fitch Plaza
Trenton, NJ 08625
(609) 292-2323

**New Mexico**
Labor and Industrial Commission
509 Camino De Los Merquez
Santa Fe, NM 87501
(505) 827-2756

**New York**
Department of Labor
State Campus
Building 12
Albany, NY 12240
(518) 457-5519

## STATE LABOR DEPARTMENTS
(continued)

**North Carolina**
Department of Labor
Labor Building
Raleigh, NC 27611
(919) 733-7166

**North Dakota**
Department of Labor
State Capitol
Bismarck, ND 58505
(701) 224-2660

**Ohio**
Department of Industrial Relations
2323 West 5th Avenue
Columbus, OH 43204
(614) 481-3685

**Oklahoma**
Department of Labor
State Capitol
Oklahoma City, OK 73105
(405) 521-2461

**Oregon**
Bureau of Labor
Labor and Industry Building
Salem, OR 97310
(503) 229-5735

**Pennsylvania**
Department of Labor and Industry
Labor and Industry Building
Harrisburg, PA 17120
(717) 783-8944

**Rhode Island**
Department of Labor
220 Elmwood Avenue
Providence, RI 02907
(401) 277-2741

**South Carolina**
Department of Labor
3600 Forest Drive
Columbia, SC 29204
(803) 758-2851

**South Dakota**
Department of Labor
Kneip Building
Pierre, SD 57501
(605) 773-3101

# STATE LABOR DEPARTMENTS
(continued)

**Tennessee**
Department of Labor
Union Building
Nashville, TN 37219
(615) 741-2582

**Texas**
Department of Labor and Standards
Thompson State Office Building
Austin, TX 78701
(512) 475-0641

**Utah**
Industry and Labor Commission
350 East 500 South Street
Salt Lake City, UT 84111
(801) 530-6801

**Vermont**
Department of Labor and Industry
State Office Building
Montpelier, VT 05602
(802) 828-2286

**Virginia**
Department of Labor and Industry
Fourth Street Office Building
Richmond, VA 23261
(804) 786-2376

**Washington**
Department of Labor and Industries
General Administration Building
Olympia, WA 98504
(206) 753-6341

**West Virginia**
Department of Labor
State Office Building
Charleston, WV 25305
(304) 348-7890

**Wisconsin**
Department of Industry
Labor and Human Relations
PO Box 7946
Madison, WI 53707
(608) 266-3131

**Wyoming**
Department of Labor and Statistics
Herschler Building
Cheyenne, WY 82002
(307) 777-7261

# STATE GOVERNMENT

*The Book of the States* is the standard reference volume on state government. You will find in this comprehensive book almost anything you need to know about your state including the names of the very top officials. Broad subjects covered are: state constitutions, state executive branches, state legislative branches, state judicial branches, state elections, state finances, state management and administration, selected state activities, issues, and services, intergovernment affairs, and a final chapter which contains a variety of statistics and information about each state. Most public libraries have a copy in their reference department.

**Suggested Reference**

*The Book of the States*, Lexington, KY, Council of State Governments, annual.
**Note:** Many states issue manuals of their own. Inquire at your public library.

## STATISTICS

Sooner or later you will probably need to locate some type of statistics. Many businesses could not plan or operate profitably without first making accurate statistical analyses based on data obtained from reliable outside sources. Judgment must enter into the use of statistics when doing research. Benjamin Disraeli once said, "There are three kinds of lies: lies, damned lies and statistics." It is imperative that you know what you are doing when you use statistics. Questions you might consider include: Who compiled them? Where did they come from? Why were they collected? Could they have been slanted to prove a point? How authoritative is the source?

Countless sources constantly issue statistics, many of which are of no interest or use to the average businessman. The statistical reference sources mentioned below are the principal ones which may help answer your needs when you seek specialized data.

### Suggested References

The three most popular and useful reference sources which contain a variety of statistics are: *The World Almanac, The Information Please Almanac* and the *Statistical Abstract of the United States.* If you do not own either of the almanacs it would be wise to invest a few dollars in one of them for each contains a wealth of information and to a great extent duplicates the other. You can probably use the *Statistical Abstract* in your library.

Bureau of the Census, *Statistical Abstract of the United States.* Washington, DC, Superintendent of Documents, annual.

*Information Please Almanac.* Boston, Houghton Mifflin, annual.

*The World Almanac and Book of Facts.* New York, World Almanac, annual.

Gale Research Company publishes two helpful statistical indexes you may find in a nearby library:

*Encyclopedia of Business Information Sources.* Detroit, Gale, published every three to five years.

*Statistics Sources.* Detroit, Gale, published every five to seven years.

Other sources for statistics are individual yearbooks for each of the states. Ask a reference librarian to help you locate what you are seeking.

## STATISTICS (continued)

Professional and trade associations also issue reports, many keep statistics, and some publish statistical studies. If the appropriate association you need to contact does not appear in the index to this book, consult Gale's *Encyclopedia of Associations.*

There are countless other possibilities for locating statistics you may need. Your best procedure is to discuss your problem with the reference librarian at the public library. If there is no library near you, contact the State Library at your state capitol and ask for help.

### Other Suggested Readings

Conover, W.J. and Ronald Iman, *Introduction to Modern Business Statistics.* New York, John Wiley and Sons, 1983.

Freund, John E. and Frank J. Williams, *Elementary Business Statistics: The Modern Approach.* Englewood Cliffs, NJ, Prentice-Hall, 1982.

Horowitz, Lois, *Knowing Where to Look: The Ultimate Guide to Research.* Cincinnati, Writer's Digest Books, 1984.

Kohler, Heinz, *Statistics for Business and Economics.* Glenview, IL, Scott, Foresman, 1985.

Mention should be made of the American Statistical Association although it issues no publications of interest to the average businessman, nor is it a source of information of statistical resources. Instead, its activities concern principally professionals who have interest in the theory and application of statistics. The association publishes a number of periodicals and proceedings, a list of which is available on request.

### For Further Information

American Statistical Association
806 15th Street, NW
Washington, DC 20005
Phone: 202-393-3253

# STOCK EXCHANGES

Initially the stock of new corporations may be traded on the "over-the-counter market," it being classified as "unlisted" stock. The stock cannot be listed on an exchange until the company is able to satisfy the listing requirements of one of the stock exchanges. This means that the company must meet certain financial qualifications, and have a sufficient number of stockholders and outstanding shares of stock to meet the minimum listing rules. Some corporations prefer to list the stock on one of the regional exchanges first. These are the Boston, Cincinnati, Intermountain, Mid-West, Pacific, Philadelphia and Spokane stock exchanges. Others prefer to begin by listing on the American Stock Exchange which has traditionally been considered a "seasoning exchange" for many stocks which eventually move over to the "Big Board," the New York Stock Exchange.

For details about an exchange's listing requirements, write to the Department of Stock List at one of the following exchanges.

**For Further Information**

American Stock Exchange
86 Trinity Place
New York, NY 10006-1818
Phone: 212-938-6000

Boston Stock Exchange
1 Boston Place
Boston, MA 02108-4499
Phone: 617-523-5625

Cincinnati Stock Exchange
49 East 4th Street
Cincinnati, OH 45202-3892
Phone: 513-621-1410

Intermountain Stock Exchange
3735 Main Street
Salt Lake City, UT 84111-2705
Phone: 801-363-2531

Midwest Stock Exchange
120 South LaSalle Street
Chicago, IL 60603-3402
Phone: 312-368-2222

New York Stock Exchange
11 Wall Street
New York, NY 10005-1916
Phone: 212-623-3000

# STOCK EXCHANGES (continued)

Pacific Stock Exchange
301 Pine Street
San Francisco, CA 94104-3301
Phone: 415-393-4000
Also at 618 South Spring Street
Los Angeles, CA 90014
Phone: 213-977-4500

Philadelphia Stock Exchange
1900 Market Street
Philadelphia, PA 19103-3527
Phone: 215-496-5000

Spokane Stock Exchange
225 Peyton Building
Spokane, WA 99201
Phone: 509-624-4632

**See also:** CORPORATE SECRETARY FUNCTIONS

## TAXES

A number of tax services and independent accountants prepare income taxes for individuals and companies. They are listed in the yellow pages of your telephone directory under "Tax Return Preparation." Some community colleges and vocational schools offer courses in tax preparation.

The IRS offers Small Business Tax Workshops designed to explain how federal taxes relate to business. The workshop introduces business taxes and highlights tax benefits and obligations connected with small business. Write the Small Business Administration, Washington, DC 20416 and request a copy of "Small Business Tax Workshop," IRS Publication 1057. Municipal, county, and state tax offices will answer questions and assist taxpayers short of preparing returns. Toll free numbers for obtaining assistance from the IRS are listed at the rear of every tax instruction booklet.

Bookstores carry a number of inexpensive federal tax guides which are revised annually to include the latest changes in the tax code. Probably the best known are J.K.Lasser's, the Arthur Young, and the H. & R. Block guides.

## TELEPHONE–800 NUMBER

In 1987 AT&T introduced an affordable 800 number service which was aimed at small businesses which wanted to be able to offer this convenience to their customers. It does not require a special telephone line or installation and can be programmed to cover only selective interstate geographic areas to meet a business's needs. Price savings are based on time of day, day of week, and call volume discount.

**For Further Information**

Call 1-800-272-0400 or ask the business office of the long distance telephone company you use if comparable service is available.

## TELEPHONE SERVICE

One business necessity which is becoming increasingly expensive is telephone service. With deregulation, local service options and a choice of long distance service in many areas, to say nothing of other choices one must make, it is important to understand what is what.

The federal government has prepared a cooperative publication developed by three federal agencies and the Bell Atlantic Companies which was also reviewed by six consumer and telephone associations. It is free for the asking.

### Reference Pamphlet

*A Consumer's Guide to Telephone Service.* Write to: Consumer Information Center, Pueblo, CO 81009.

## TEMPORARY EMPLOYEES

There are numerous employment agencies which contract with businesses to supply personnel needed on a temporary basis. Such temporary employees are hired and employed by the employment contractor who pays the employee, performs all necessary payroll deductions and tax reporting, thus saving the business which contracts for the employee this trouble and expense. In some instances temporary employees are bonded.

For the names of employment agencies which specialize in contracting temporary employees, consult the yellow pages of your phone directory under "Employment Contractor—Temporary Help" or a similar heading.

### Suggested Reference

Smith, Demaris C., *Temporary Employment—The Flexible Alternative.* White Hall, VA, Betterway Publications, 1986

## TIME ZONES

The relation of time as a person travels east or west became so confusing to the young railroads that in 1883 our present time zone system was introduced. Should you need to know in which time zone a city or town in the United States is located, consult your phone directory. Most books contain a map showing all area codes as well as the boundry lines of the Atlantic, Eastern, Central, Mountain and Pacific time zones. This is usually found in the front matter of the white pages of a phone book.

For international time zones, consult the maps which appear in both the *Information Please Almanac* and the *World Almanac.*

In computing time differences, be sure to take into account daylight saving time which starts the first Sunday in April and ends with the last Sunday in October. Some states and territories have voted to exempt themselves from going on Daylight Saving Time. They are: Arizona, Hawaii, part of Indiana, Puerto Rico, the Virgin Islands and American Samoa.

## TOLL–FREE TELEPHONE DIRECTORY

A useful directory of toll-free numbers you can call, in fact 35,000 of them—including a special hotel-motel section—is the *Toll-Free Digest,* published in Claverack, NY by the Toll-Free Digest Co., annual.

A smaller toll-free listing is contained also in the *National Directory of Addresses and Telephone Numbers.*

**See also:** NATIONAL TELEPHONE DIRECTORY

# TRADEMARKS

A trademark is made up of distinctive word, name, symbol or device used by manufacturers, merchants and businessmen to identify their goods or services and distinguish them from those manufactured or sold by others. Trademarks which are registered for 20 years with renewal rights, are examined by the Patent and Trademark Office for compliance with various laws to prevent unfair competition and consumer deception.

## For Further Information

Commissioner of Patents and Trademarks
Patent and Trademark Office
Washington, DC 20231
Phone: 703-557-3341
Note: Operations are conducted at 2021 Jefferson Davis Highway, Arlington, VA.

## Suggested Reference

Diamond, Sidney A., *Trademark Problems and How to Avoid Them.* Chicago, Crain Books, 1981.

Reid, Brian C., *A Practical Introduction to Trade Marks.* Elmsford, NY, Pergamon, 1984.

U.S. Trademark Association, *Trademark Management: A Guide for Businessmen.* New York, Boardman, 1981.

# TRANSPORTATION SCHEDULES

Those who travel frequently and use various forms of transportation usually must plan their trips in advance and need to consult bus, plane or train schedules. A travel agency can provide schedule information and make reservations. If one is not handy, it should be possible to contact an agency by phone and obtain the information you need as well as make reservations in advance, paying by credit card or check.

Amtrak publishes some schedules which are obtainable by writing Amtrack, Six Penn Center Plaza, Philadelphia, PA 19103. Schedules for airlines, buses, and steamships are published in the guides listed below. They may be consulted at some large public and university libraries, air and bus terminals and at some agencies which sell bus tickets and provide passenger ticket services.

## Suggested References

*Official Airline Guide.* Oak Brook, IL, Official Airline Guides, bi-weekly.

Official *Steamship Guide International.* New Canaan, CT, Transportation Guides, monthly.

*Russell's Official National Motor Coach Guide* (U.S. Mexico, Canada). Cedar Rapids, IA, Russell's Guides, monthly.

Of possible interest if one is traveling abroad, is *Jane's World Railways 1986–1987.* New York, Jane's Publishing, annual.

## TRUTH–IN–LENDING LAW

The Truth-in-Lending Act is one part of the Consumer Credit Protection Act. It was designed to protect consumers and enable them to shop intelligently for the best interest rates and terms when they seek credit. The two most important features of the law are those which require the lender to give information about the finance charge in a dollar amount, and also as an annual percentage rate. The law applies to all who extend credit to individuals for agricultural, family, household or personal purposes and includes auto dealers, finance companies, banks, credit unions, savings and loan associations, retail stores, credit card companies, mortgage bankers, dentists, doctors, electricians, plumbers, carpenters and the like, if they extend credit regularly.

The Fair Credit Reporting Act, another part of the Consumer Credit Protection Act, insures that consumer reporting activities are conducted in a fair and equitable manner, upholding the consumer's right to privacy and giving the consumer several important other rights.

### For Further Information

Director
Office of Public Information
Federal Trade Commission
Washington, DC 20580
Phone: 202-523-3598

### Suggested Reference

The Federal Reserve System issues a number of pamphlets, some dealing with truth-in-lending and the Equal Credit Opportunity Act. Copies are free, information about them may be obtained by phoning 202-452-3244.

## UNITED FUNDS

United Funds or Community Chests exist in countless cities and towns enabling the individual and businessman to make a single donation which is apportioned among all of the participating health, welfare, and other philanthropic agencies. In addition to a company donation, in-plant solicitations of employees with or without payroll deductions are permitted and encouraged by many businesses. Businessmen are sought to help manage local funds.

### For Further Information

United Way of America
701 North Fairfax Street
Alexandria, VA 22314
Phone: 703-836-7100

# USED CAR RULE

The Federal Trade Commission's new Used Car Rule may help you if you are buying a used car. The rule requires all used car dealers to place a large sticker, called a "Buyers Guide" in the window of each used vehicle they offer for sale. Dealers are required to post Buyers Guides on all used vehicles, including used automobiles, light-duty vans and light-duty trucks. Private individuals offering vehicles for sale are not covered by the rule.

The Federal Trade Commission, Bureau of Consumer Protection, Office of Consumer/Business Education has published an informative brochure explaining the Buyers Guide. It is available on request. If you have questions about the rule, you can contact the Federal Trade Commission at its Headquarters Office, 6th and Pennsylvania Avenue, NW, Washington, DC 20580. Phone: 202-376-2805.

Free FTC facts sheets on "Warranties" or "Service Contracts" may be obtained from the Public Reference Office, Federal Trade Commission, Washington, DC 20580.

# WAGE AND SALARY INFORMATION

Businessmen frequently need comparative wage and salary figures to use as yardsticks when adjusting their wage scales or hiring new employees. It is difficult to obtain this data because most companies are reluctant to disclose such information. Some firms trade wage and salary figures on a confidential basis but competing companies rarely do this.

There are several sources for this information, one or more of which may provide some helpful material. They are:

1. Proxy statements of corporations listed on a stock exchange. The law requires that the three highest salaries be reported annually. Proxy statements can be requested from the Office of the Secretary of a corporation, or seen at any regional office of the Securities & Exchange Commission.

2. Trade associations frequently compile and publish such information for the confidential use of their members.

3. Some state labor departments compile data from time to time. Ask your state labor department if it has any statistics which would be useful.

4. The Bureau of Labor Statistics compiles a number of helpful sets of statistics (See LABOR STATISTICS).

5. The Bureau of Labor Statistics issues the following publications which are available from the Superintendent of Documents, Washington, DC 20402:

*Current Wage Developments.* Monthly, subscription $21 per year, single copy $4.50.

*Employment and Earnings.* Monthly, subscription $31 per year, single copy $4.50.

*Area Wage Surveys.* 70 per year, subscription $115, a single copy varies in price.

# WEATHER INFORMATION

Many businesses require accurate and up-to-date weather information on a continuous basis. There are a number of private weather services scattered about the country but they may be difficult to find. Consult the yellow pages of your phone directory under "Weather Services" and if none are listed, contact the National Weather Association which maintains a partial listing of private weather services.

**For Further Information**

National Weather Association
4400 Stamp Road
Temple Hills, MD 20748
Phone: 301-899-3784

# WHOLESALING–DISTRIBUTING

Gale's *Encyclopedia of Associations* lists a number of trade organizations which represent wholesaler-distributors engaged in various specialized activities.

In addition, small, medium and large businesses in the wholesale-distribution business will find the activities of the National Association of Wholesaler-Distributors (NAW) of interest. The organization's membership includes thousands of individual firms and a federation of more than 100 national wholesale distribution trade associations. The association maintains Washington representation, provides various member programs and issues a number of publications of interest and value to those in the industry, discounts being offered to members. "Update," a catalog of management materials offered for sale, is available on request.

**For Further Information**

National Association of Wholesaler-Distributors
1725 K Street, NW
Washington, DC 20006
Phone: 202-872-0085

# WORD FINDERS

From time to time every businessman needs to find just the right word to express the meaning he is trying to convey. The dictionary may be of limited help but one or both of the reference books listed below should solve most problems.

An antonym is a word of an opposite meaning; a synonym, a word with the same or nearly the same meaning; and a thesaurus, a book of words and their synonyms. The most famous thesaurus is Roget's, originally compiled by the Frenchman, Peter Mark Roget, in 1852. You can find the book in its original form arranged in 20 categories, but it is also available in an alphabetical arrangement which is much easier to use. Every office should have a thesaurus to accompany the dictionary. You will find various thesauruses in a bookstore, the one we include below is based on the original.

### Suggested References

*Roget's International Thesaurus.* New York, Harper & Row.

Reader's Digest Association, *Family Word Finder, a New Thesaurus of Synonyms and Antonyms in Dictionary Form.* Pleasantville, NY, Reader's Digest Association, 1986.

# WRITER'S MARKETS

Businessmen interested in writing and placing books or articles with book or periodical publishers may find the following directories helpful:

R.R. Bowker Company, *Literary Market Place: The Directory of American Book Publishing.* New York, R.R. Bowker Company, annual.

Writer's Digest Books, *Writer's Market.* Cincinnati, Writer's Digest Books, annual.

—— *Writer's Resource Guide.* Cincinnati, Writer's Digest Books, 1983.

—— *Writer's Yearbook.* Cincinnati, Writer's Digest Books, annual.

For the titles of how-to books on writing, consult the advertisement of Writer's Digest books usually carried in the *Writer's Digest,* and the books listed under Authorship in the latest issue of *Books in Print.*

## YELLOW PAGES

If you have difficulty locating the service or product you are seeking in the yellow pages of your phone book, look under "Advertising Directory and Guide" for the phone number to call to obtain assistance or look under the index in the front of the phone book. Should you want to consider advertising in the yellow pages, the number to call is also given under these listings.

**See also:** NATIONAL TELEPHONE DIRECTORY, TOLL–FREE TELEPHONE DIRECTORY

# Part II
# Organizations

# ORGANIZATIONS

This second part of the book contains a selected list of associations (see also, ASSOCIATIONS, in Part I). These organizations were chosen because they represent some of the principal areas of interest or concern to the average business, especially when undertaking an initial investigation of a problem or topic relating to health, personnel, research, marketing, production, government regulation, etc. By contacting the appropriate agency it should be possible to obtain either the information sought or a lead to the best source.

When writing government agencies, address your inquiry to the Office of Information and Public Affairs; when writing private organizations, address your letter to the Public Relations Department. All non-governmental organizations will appreciate your enclosing a stamped self-addressed envelope. This is important because most non-profit agencies have limited funds for postage.

Be sure to check the index if you do not find a subject listed here. Organizations mentioned in Part I are not repeated in this listing.

**Abrasives**
Abrasive Engineering Society
1700 Painters Run Road
Pittsburgh, PA 15243

**Aerospace**
American Institute of Aeronautics and
    Astronautics
1633 Broadway
New York, NY 10019

**Aerospace Industries**
Aerospace Industries Association of America
1725 De Sales Street, NW
Washington, DC 20036

**Agriculture**
American Farm Bureau Federation
225 Touhy Avenue
Park Ridge, IL 60068

U.S. Department of Agriculture
Washington, DC 20250

**Air Conditioning**
Air Conditioning and Refrigeration Institute
1501 Wilson Boulevard
Arlington, VA 22209

# ORGANIZATIONS (continued)

**Air Force**
U.S. Department of the Air Force
The Pentagon
Washington, DC 20330

**Air Freight**
Air Freight Association of America
1730 Rhode Island Avenue, NW
Washington, DC 20036

**Air Pollution**
Air Pollution Control Association
PO Box 2861
Pittsburgh, PA 15230

U.S. Environmental Protection Agency
Washington, DC 20460

**Air Taxis**
National Air Transportation Association
4226 King Street
Alexandria, VA 22302

**Air Transportation**
Air Transport Association of America
1709 New York Avenue, NW
Washington, DC 20006

**Airports**
Airport Operators Council International
1700 K Street, NW
Washington, DC 20006

**Aluminum**
The Aluminum Association
818 Connecticut Avenue, NW
Washington, DC 20006

**American Legion**
American Legion
P.O. Box 1055
Indianapolis, IN 46206

**Appliances**
Association of Home Appliances Manufacturers
20 North Wacker Drive
Chicago, IL 60606

**Appraising (Property)**
American Society of Appraisers
11800 Sunrise Valley Drive
Reston, VA 22091

**Architecture**
American Institute of Architects
1735 New York Avenue, NW
Washington, DC 20006

## ORGANIZATIONS (continued)

**Army**
U.S. Department of the Army
The Pentagon
Washington, DC 20310

**Art**
American Federation of Arts
41 East 65 Street
New York, NY 10021

**Arthritis**
The Arthritis Foundation
1314 Spring Street, NW
Atlanta, GA 30309

**Asphalt**
Asphalt Institute
Asphalt Institute Building
College Park, MD 20740

**Audio-Visual Equipment**
International Communications Industries
    Association
3150 Spring Street
Fairfax, VA 22031

**Automobiles**
Motor Vehicle Manufacturers Association of the
    United States
300 New Center Building
Detroit, MI 48202

**Aviation**
U.S. Federal Aviation Administration
Washington, DC 20591

**Banking**
American Bankers Association
1120 Connecticut Avenue, NW
Washington, DC 20036

**Beverages**
National Soft Drink Association
1101-16 Street, NW
Washington, DC 20036

**Biological Sciences**
American Institute of Biological Science
1401 Wilson Boulevard
Arlington, VA 22209

**Blindness**
American Foundation for the Blind
15 West 16th Street
New York, NY 10011

## ORGANIZATIONS (continued)

**Book Publishing**
Association of American Publishers
1 Park Avenue
New York, NY 10016

**Bookselling**
American Booksellers Association
122 East 42 Street
New York, NY 10168

**Broadcasting**
National Association of Broadcasters
1771 N Street, NW
Washington, DC 20036

**Business Aircraft**
National Business Aircraft Association
1634 I Street, NW
Washington, DC 20004

**Business Counselors**
Institute of Certified Business Counselors
3301 Vincent Road
Pleasant Hill, CA 94523

**Cancer**
American Cancer Society
90 Park Avenue
New York, NY 10017

**Cement**
Portland Cement Association
Old Orchard Road
Skokie, IL 60076

**Ceramics**
American Ceramic Society
65 Ceramic Drive
Columbus, OH 43214

**Chemistry**
American Chemical Society
1155-16 Street, NW
Washington, DC 20036

**Chiropractic**
American Chiropractors Association
1916 Wilson Boulevard
Arlington, VA 22201

**Civil Liberties**
American Civil Liberties Union
132 West 43 Street
New York, NY 10036

**Civil Rights**
Civil Rights Division
U.S. Department of Justice
Washington, DC 20530

## ORGANIZATIONS (continued)

**Coast Guard**
U.S. Coast Guard
Washington, DC 20590

**Communications**
U.S. Federal Communications Commission
Washington, DC 20554

**Conservation**
National Wildlife Federation
1412-16 Street, NW
Washington, DC 20036

U.S. Fish and Wildlife Service
Washington, DC 20240

**Construction**
Associated Builders and Contractors
729-15 Street, NW
Washington, DC 20005

Associated General Contractors of America
1957 E Street, NW
Washington, DC 20006

**Cystic Fibrosis**
Cystic Fibrosis Foundation
6000 Executive Boulevard
Rockville, MD 20852

**Dentistry**
American Dental Association
211 East Chicago Avenue
Chicago, IL 60611

**Diabetes**
American Diabetes Association
1660 Duke Street
Alexandria, VA 22314

**Direct Mail**
Direct Marketing Association
6 East 43rd Street
New York, NY 10017

**Economics**
American Economic Associations
1313-21 Avenue South
Nashville, TN 37212

**Electric Power**
Bureau of Reclamation
U.S. Department of the Interior
Washington, DC 20240

Edison Electric Institute
1111-19 Street, NW
Washington, DC 20036

## ORGANIZATIONS (continued)

U.S. Department of Energy
Washington, DC 20585

U.S. Rural Electrification Administration
U.S. Department of Agriculture
Washington, DC 20250

U.S. Nuclear Regulatory Commission
Washington, DC 20555

**Electric Utilities**
Edison Electric Institute
1111-19 Street, NW
Washington, DC 20036

**Electrical Manufacturing**
National Electrical Manufacturers Association
2101 L Street, NW
Washington, DC 20007

**Electronics**
Electronics Industries Association
2001 Eye Street, NW
Washington, DC 20006

**Engineering**
National Society of Professional Engineers
2029 K Street, NW
Washington, DC 20006

**Engineering-Chemical**
American Institute of Chemical Engineers
345 East 47 Street
New York, NY 10017

**Engineering-Civil**
American Society of Civil Engineers
345 East 47 Street
New York, NY 10017

**Engineering-Industrial**
Institute of Industrial Engineers, Inc.
25 Technology Park
Atlanta, GA 30092

**Engineering-Mechanical**
American Society of Mechanical Engineers
345 East 47 Street
New York, NY 10017

**Engineering-Metallurgical**, see Engineering-
Mining

## ORGANIZATIONS (continued)

**Engineering-Mining**
American Institute of Mining
Metallurgical and Petroleum Engineers
345 East 47th Street
New York, NY 10017

**Engineering-Petroleum,** see Engineering-Mining

**Engineering-Plastics**
Society of Plastics Engineers
14 Fairfield Drive
Brookfield Drive
Brookfield Center, CT 06805

**Engineering-Professional**
National Society of Professional Engineers
1420 King Street
Alexandria, VA 22314

**Engineering Societies**
American Association of Engineering Societies
345 East 47th Street
New York, NY 10017

**Farming**
U.S. Department of Agriculture
Washington, DC 20250

**Federal Reserve System**
U.S. Federal Reserve System
Washington, DC 20551

**Firearms**
National Rifle Association
1600 Rhode Island Avenue, NW
Washington, DC 20036

**Fixed Based Operators,** see Air Taxis

**Foreign Trade**
U.S. Tariff Commission
Washington, DC 20436

**Forestry**
U.S. Forest Service
U.S. Department of Agriculture
Washington, DC 20013

**Graphic Arts**
Graphic Arts Technical Foundation
4615 Forbes Avenue
Pittsburgh, PA 15213

**History**
American Association for State and Local History
708 Berry Road
Nashville, TN 37204

## ORGANIZATIONS (continued)

**House Organs**
International Association of Business
    Communicators
870 Market Street
San Francisco, CA 94102

**Housing**
U.S. Department of Housing and Urban
    Development
Washington, DC 20410

**Illumination**
Illuminating Engineering Society
345 East 47th Street
New York, NY 10017

**Immigration**
U.S. Immigration and Naturalization Service
Washington, DC 20536

**Insulation**
National Insulation Contractors Association
1025 Vermont Avenue, NW
Washington, DC 20005

**Insurance-Health**
Health Insurance Association of America
1850 K Street, NW
Washington, DC 20523

**Libraries**
American Library Association
50 East Huron Street
Chicago, IL 60611

**Machine Tools**
National Machine Tool Builders
7901 Westpark Drive
McLean, VA 22102

Tool and Dye Institute
777 Busse Highway
Park Ridge, IL 60068

**Manufacturers**
National Association of Manufacturers
1776 F Street, NW
Washington, DC 20006

**Mapping**
American Congress on Surveying and Mapping
210 Little Falls
Falls Church, VA 22046

**Marine Corps**
U.S. Marine Corps
The Pentagon
Washington, DC 20390

## ORGANIZATIONS (continued)

**Materials Handling**
International Material Management Society
650 East Higgins Road
Schaumburg, IL 60195

**Medical Problems**
American Medical Association
535 North Dearborn Street
Chicago, IL 60610

**Medicare**
U.S. Department of Health, Education and
   Welfare
Washington, DC 20201

**Mental Health**
National Association for Mental Health
1021 Prince Street
Alexandria, VA 22314

**Monopoly**
U.S. Federal Trade Commission
Washington, DC 20580

**Motor Carriers**
U.S. Interstate Commerce Commission
Washington, DC 20580

**Motors and Equipment**
Motor and Equipment Manufacturers Association
222 Cedar Lane, Teaneck, NJ 07666

**Multiple Sclerosis**
National Multiple Sclerosis Society
205 East 42nd Street
New York, NY 10017

**Muscular Dystrophy**
Muscular Dystrophy Association of America
810-7th Avenue
New York, NY 10019

**Natural Gas**
U.S. Department of Energy
Washington, DC 20585

**Navy**
U.S. Department of the Navy
The Pentagon
Washington, DC 20350

**Nuclear Energy**
American Nuclear Society
555 North Kensington Avenue
LaGrange Park, IL 60625

U.S. Nuclear Regulatory Commission
Washington, DC 20555

## ORGANIZATIONS (continued)

**Nursing**
National League for Nursing
10 Columbus Circle
New York, NY 10019

**Nutrition**
American Dietetic Association
430 North Michigan Avenue
Chicago, IL 60611

**Oil Pipe Lines**
Association of Oil Pipe Lines
1725 K Street, NW
Washington, DC 20006

**Optics**
Optical Society of America
1816 Jefferson Place, NW
Washington, DC 20036

**Optometry**
American Optometric Association
243 North Lindbergh Boulevard
St. Louis, MO 63141

**Osteopathy**
American Osteopathic Association
212 East Ohio Street
Chicago, IL 60611

**Paper**
American Paper Institute
260 Madison Avenue
New York, NY 10016

**Pension Plans**
Association of Private Pension and Welfare Plans
1331 Pennsylvania Avenue
Washington, DC 20001

**Planning**
American Planning Association
1776 Massachusetts Avenue, NW
Washington, DC 20036

**Podiatry**
American Podiatric Medical Association
20 Chevy Chase Circle
Washington, DC 20015

**Political Science**
American Academy of Political and
   Social Science
3937 Chestnut Street
Philadelphia, PA 19104

## ORGANIZATIONS (continued)

**Population**
Population Association of America
806-15 Street, NW
Washington, DC 20005

**Psychology**
American Psychological Association
1200-17 Street, NW
Washington, DC 20036

**Public Accountants**
American Institute of Certified Public
   Accountants
1211 Avenue of the Americas
New York, NY 10036

**Public Health**
American Public Health Association
1015-15 Street, NW
Washington, DC 20005

U.S. Public Health Service
Washington, DC 20201

**Race Relations**
B'nai B'rith International
1640 Rhode Island Avenue, NW
Washington, DC 20036

National Association for the Advancement of
Colored People
186 Remsen Street
Brooklyn, NY 11201

National Council of Churches
475 Riverside Drive
New York, NY 10115

**Railroads**
Association of American Railroads
50 F Street, NW
Washington, DC 20001

U.S. Interstate Commerce Commission
Washington, DC 20423

**Real Estate**
National Association of Realtors
430 North Michigan Avenue
Chicago, IL 60611

**Red Cross**
American Red Cross
17 and D Streets, NW
Washington, DC 20006

**Refrigeration,** see Air Conditioning

## ORGANIZATIONS (continued)

**Rehabilitation**
National Rehabilitation Association
633 South Washington Street
Alexandria, VA 22314

**Retailing**
American Retail Federation
1616 H Street, NW
Washington, DC 20006

**Rubber**
Rubber Manufacturers Association
1400 K Street, NW
Washington, DC 20005

**Savings Banks**
National Council of Savings Institutions
1101-15 Street, NW
Washington, DC 20005

**Securities Regulation**
U.S. Securities & Exchange Commission
Washington, DC 20549

**Selling**
Sales and Marketing Executives-International
6151 Wilson Mills Road
Cleveland, OH 44143

**Shipping**
American Bureau of Shipping
45 Eisenhower Drive
Paramus, NJ 07652

U.S. Federal Maritime Commission
Washington, DC 20573

**Soap**
The Soap and Detergent Association
475 Park Avenue South
New York, NY 10016

**Social Science**
American Academy of Political and Social
   Science
3937 Chestnut Street
Philadelphia, PA 19104

**Soil Conservation**
Soil Science Society of America
677 South Segoe Road
Madison, WI 53711

U.S. Soil Conservation Service
U.S. Department of Agriculture
Washington, DC 20013

**Surveying,** see Mapping

# ORGANIZATIONS (continued)

**Tariffs**
U.S. Tariff Commission
Washington, DC 20436

**Taxes**
Tax Foundation, Inc.
1 Thomas Circle, NW
Washington, DC 20005

**Technical Schools**
National Association of Trade and Technical
    Schools
2021 K Street, NW
Washington, DC 20006

**Textiles**
American Textile Manufacturers Institute
1101 Connecticut Avenue, NW
Washington, DC 20036

**Trade Schools,** see Technical Schools

**Vocational Training,** see Technical Schools

**Water Pollution**
U.S. Environmental Protection Agency
Washington, DC 20460

Water Pollution Control Federation
2626 Pennsylvania Avenue, NW
Washington, DC 20037

**Waterworks**
American Water Works Association
6666 West Quincy Avenue
Denver, CO 80235

**Welding**
American Welding Society
550 NW LeJeune Road
Miami, FL 33126

**Wool**
The Wool Bureau, 360 Lexington Avenue
New York, NY 10017

# Appendices

# GLOSSARY OF BUSINESS AND FINANCIAL TERMS

**Automatic Stabilizers** — those federal government expenditures and receipts which automatically increase or decrease without action being taken by the President or the Congress are known as automatic stabilizers. The principal government expenditures which rise or fall automatically as economic conditions change are unemployment compensation payments and subsidies paid farmers. Similarly the government's principal income, the income tax paid by corporations and individuals, rises and falls as incomes increase or decrease.

**Balance of Payments** — A record of all financial transactions which take place between the United States and the rest of the world. It covers payments and receipts for private and governmental transactions. A country has a balance-of-payments deficit when its international payments are greater than its international receipts, and a favorable balance of payments when the reverse is true.

**Bear Market** — This refers to a time when prices on the stock exchange are falling.

**Bilateral Monopoly** — A term which refers to a labor market in which one labor union has a monopoly because all the workers qualified to work in a certain industry are members of the same union.

**Black Market** — When the government rations and/or fixes prices at which various scarce goods may be sold, those who sell goods illegally at such a time are said to be operating a black market. A gray market describes the practice of selling scarce goods secretly above prevailing prices when this practice is not forbidden by the government. Such sales are unethical but not illegal.

**Blue Sky Laws** — These are laws enacted by various states to regulate the sale of securities within the states.

**Bull Market** — Refers to a time when prices on the stock exchange are rising.

**Business Cycles** — Swings in business activity from peak periods which bring prosperity to lows which accompany depressions.

**Capital** — A term meaning wealth, excepting land which produces more wealth. Most of the assets used in a business are considered capi-

# GLOSSARY OF BUSINESS AND FINANCIAL TERMS (continued)

tal because they generate wealth. Money people save is capital if it is invested to earn interest or dividends.

**Capital Gains** — Profit resulting from the sale of capital investments such as stocks and bonds, real estate, business enterprises, etc.

**Capitalism** — Capitalism is an economic system in which the means of production and the distribution of goods are mostly privately owned and operated for private profit. A capitalist, therefore, is an owner of capital or one who has a large amount of money invested in a business.

**Cartel** — A cartel is an association of independent financial or industrial companies in the same business or similar fields, formed to influence the market by regulating competition. It is regulated competition rather than free competition.

**Collective Bargaining** — This is the right of workers who have organized a union to negotiate collectively with their employer. The Wagner Act reaffirmed the collective bargaining provision of the National Industrial Recovery Act, which was approved in 1933 and included such a provision.

**Competition** — Competition is the rivalry found in business between individuals and/or companies trying to win the same markets. The old saying: "Competition is the life of trade" infers that each company must do its best in order to win and keep customers for its goods or services.

**Conglomerate** — A term coined during the 1960s to describe the giant enterprises created by business mergers when many corporations purchased a number of companies which had no relation to each other. The reason behind the wave of mergers was the desire to diversify and hopefully acquire companies whose operations would add to the parent corporation's profits.

**Consumerism** — A fairly new word coined to describe what has been called a consumer revolution. The old motto "Let the buyer beware" became "Let the seller beware." Although many states had bureaus offering consumer protection, the federal government

## GLOSSARY OF BUSINESS AND FINANCIAL TERMS (continued)

took the lead in passing legislation to help protect consumers.

**Credit Crunch** — A credit crunch occurs when credit is not available to many businesses and individuals as has been the case in the past.

**Currency** — Our current medium of exchange known as currency consists of both paper bills and metal coins. The amount of currency in circulation varies, depending on how much the public requires. When money is not needed it flows back into the banks in the form of deposits.

**Deficit Financing** — This term refers to a government's practice of borrowing money required to pay for goods and services for which no cash is available in the treasury.

**Demand Deposits** — These are deposits of money in a bank account which the depositor may withdraw without giving advance notice.

**Deflation** — Deflation is the opposite of inflation and usually results when industry cannot sell its goods profitably. Business activity declines, workers are laid off, and a dollar buys more goods and services as prices fall rapidly. When a period of deflation becomes severe it is called a recession or depression.

**Discretionary Income** — This refers to the income remaining after an individual or family has provided for food, clothing and shelter.

**Economic Indicators** — The financial sections of some newspapers report the latest trends as shown by many economic indicators. These consist of special price indexes and reports, the following being among the most important: Business Failures, Business Inventories, Carloadings Reports, Consumer Credit Reports, Consumer Price Index, Dow Jones Industrial Average, Gross National Product, Money in Circulation, Personal Income, and Retail Trade.

**Entrepreneur** — The *entrepreneur* is a person who decides to start a business, expand a company, buy an existing firm or perhaps borrow money to manufacture a new product or offer a new service. He or she is the most important person in our free enterprise system because the entrepreneur is the manager and the risk taker.

**Excise Tax** — This refers to taxes on the manufacture or sale of various commodities such as liquor, tobacco, automobiles, safe deposit box rents, electrical energy, and so forth.

**Fair Return** — This term refers to the profits which a public utility may earn. The law has established the principle that a public utility may charge a rate which is sufficient to earn a reasonable return on the money it has prudently invested in the company, provided the utility is operated in a proper manner. At the same time the rates charged must be reasonable too.

**Featherbedding** — The word featherbedding is said to have originated in the railroad industry when some trainmen complained about the condition of the mattresses in their caboose. The irate trainmaster asked: "What do you brakemen want — feather beds?"

The term now applies to those work rules which require the employment of more workers than needed for the job. In addition, when technological advances eliminate positions, unions often insist that the workers be retained and receive their regular pay for doing nothing.

**Fiat Money** — Fiat money consists of paper notes which the government prints and makes legal tender. Since there is no gold or silver on deposit in the federal treasury, it cannot be redeemed for any valuable metal.

**Fiscal Policy** — This term broadly refers to the manner in which our federal government levies and collects taxes, purchases its goods and services, spends its funds and manages the national debt.

**Fixed Capital** — Fixed capital refers to things like airplanes, trucks, machinery, power plants and buildings which are used to create more wealth by producing goods or services.

**Free Enterprise** — This is an economic system based on the private ownership and operation of business with a minimum of governmental control. Free enterprise, also known as private enterprise, assumes that individuals own and control their own goods and labor, operate in a free market and have competition. In this system there is no place for cartels, monopolies, or government regulation.

**Free Trade** — This term usually refers to international trade which is free of govern-

## GLOSSARY OF BUSINESS AND FINANCIAL TERMS (continued)

ment regulations as well as import or export duties.

**Fringe Benefits** — This refers to benefits an employer gives his workers in addition to wages. These may include paid holidays, paid vacations, pensions, life, accident and health insurance, medical examinations, free lunches and/or coffee breaks, tuition for evening courses, free transportation in the company's buses, trains, or planes, discounts on purchases of company products, free uniforms, bonuses, profit sharing, stock purchase plans, incentive pay plans, washup time, travel time, etc.

**Golden Parachute** — When a company is threatened by a takeover, the executives may be given special employment and severance contracts. These are known as a "golden parachute."

**Gross National Product** — This term is used to measure the total value of all the goods and services produced in the country during the year. The official statistics of the federal government divide the GNP into four parts: Consumer Purchases, Business Investor Purchases, Government Purchases and Net Exports of Goods and Services. Each of these classifications is broken down into numerous subdivisions, making it possible to find out how much consumers and government spend on various goods and services.

**Guaranteed Annual Wage** — This is an agreement wherein an employer promises to pay his workers all or part of their regular wages even if the plant is closed. This term should not be confused with the term *guaranteed income* which refers to one possible solution to the poverty problem. Guaranteed income would give unemployed, part-time workers, or those paid sub-standard wages a minimum income-floor for every family.

**Holding Company** — This term refers to a company that owns enough stock of another company to control its policies and operation. Corporations so owned and controlled are called subsidiaries. If a company gains control of two or more holding companies, the practice is called "pyramiding." This type of organiza-

tion has been popular among public utilities, banks and some manufacturing concerns.

**Inflation** — Inflation refers to a period when prices climb because the supply of goods is not large enough to satisfy the public's purchasing power or demand. As prices rise during an inflationary period, money loses its value, companies may expand and earn larger profits and some people may have extra cash to spend. At the same time workers demand higher and higher wages to keep up with inflated living costs. The increased wages, however, only add to the workers' purchasing power and raise prices again, thus creating an inflationary "wage-price spiral."

Deflation is the opposite of inflation and usually results when industry cannot sell its goods profitably. Business activity declines, workers are laid off, and the dollar buys more goods and services, while prices fall rapidly.

**Interest** — This is the price a lender charges for the use of money. It is based on the idea that a person who lends to another is entitled to a profit for the use of his money. Interest is calculated as part of a percentage of the whole amount of money to be borrowed and is always expressed in percentages. Interest rates are determined primarily by the law of supply and demand. When money is scarce interest rates rise but decline when money is plentiful.

**Journeymen** — A journeyman is a skilled tradesman or an artisan who has completed an organized and recognized apprenticeship program. An apprenticeship program permits apprentices to study a trade while working and at the end of a certain period to qualify as a journeyman.

**Laissez-Faire** — A term popularized by the French philosopher, Francois Quesnay, to mean let (people) do (as they please) or *let things alone.* The French economist, Jean Claude Marie Vincent Gournay (1712–1759) originated the term as "laissez-faire, laissez-passer" (leave people alone, let goods pass freely). He believed those who produced wealth should be free to act as they wished and compete with each other without interference. Adam Smith advocated laizzez-faire in his *Wealth of Nations*

## GLOSSARY OF BUSINESS AND FINANCIAL TERMS (continued)

and the doctrine became popular in England and then in the United States.

**Lockout** — When an employer closes up his company or shop in order to keep employees from working during a strike or labor dispute, it is called a lockout.

**M-1** — This is the Federal Reserve Bank's leading money-supply statistic. It has consisted of cash and checking accounts but now also includes NOW accounts — the interest-bearing checking accounts.

**Multiplier Principle** — The word multiplier refers to the spending that is stimulated when a company has money to invest in capital improvements. When a company adds a new wing to a factory, in addition to buying building supplies and machinery, it is assumed that the management will also pay wages to the construction workers who in turn will spend the money they receive and the money will spread out thereafter in lesser and lesser amounts as it changes hands.

**NASDAQ Composite Index** — The National Association of Securities Dealers publishes eight indexes each day to assist investors in evaluating the large over-the-counter market. The NASDAQ Composite Index is a daily index of the performance of over 3,000 stocks, the majority of which are over-the-counter issues.

**Partnership** — Two or more individuals who have agreed to pool their capital, work together and share the profits and risks of conducting a business, constitute a partnership. Most partnerships are formed by brokers, lawyers, architects and other professional men and women.

**Private Sector** — This term refers to consumers and private producers who operate in the free markets as contrasted to the public sector where government agencies decide what goods (such as surplus foods) and services (such as bank deposit insurance or old-age pensions) will be provided and who may buy them.

**Proprietorship** — This term refers to a business owned and controlled by a single individual. Regardless of size, if there is one owner, the company is known as a proprietorship.

**Prospectus** — Before a public offering of stock can be made, a company must file a detailed

## GLOSSARY OF BUSINESS AND FINANCIAL TERMS (continued)

"Registration Statement" with the SEC. Incorporate in the Registration Statement is a section called the *Prospectus.* This is a report prepared for distribution to the public and it contains all the data an investor would need to help him or her decide whether or not to purchase the stock.

**Right-to-Work Laws** — Those who object to compulsory unionism believe it is contrary to our American way of life to force a person to join any kind of organization and contribute to its financial support in order to obtain employment. A union that represents a majority of a company's employees understandably feels it is not fair for non-members to share all the wage increases and other benefits which it has spent money to win. A partial solution is the "agency shop" devised to obtain financial aid from non-union members, but any union would naturally prefer a closed shop where it could represent every employee.

Many states have enacted right-to-work laws which effectively bar the closed or union shop, preferential hiring and maintenance of membership agreements between employers and unions.

**Runaway Shop** — Often a union makes wage demands which an employer is unable or unwilling to grant. When this happens and the employer closes the plant and moves his operation to another location to escape the union's jurisdiction, it is known as a runaway shop.

**Subsidy** — Today this term refers to a grant of money given by a government to a private enterprise for the benefit of the public. Today the federal government makes grants for broad categories which include agriculture, business, labor, and home-owners and tenants. Actually many other subsidy programs exist for the needy, school lunch programs, hospital operation, medical care, etc.

**Supply and Demand** — Supply is the total amount of goods or commodities which are available for purchase at a given price. Demand is not necessarily what people want to buy, but the amount of goods that people are willing and able to purchase at a certain price.

## GLOSSARY OF BUSINESS AND FINANCIAL TERMS (continued)

**Tight Money** — This expression refers to a period when the supply of credit shrinks and people find it difficult to obtain money at any price. In 1966 the Federal Reserve Board tried to halt inflation by stopping credit growth. The Board kept money scarce for about six months, creating a shortage of money which was called a "credit crunch." The Federal Reserve Board can create a tight-money condition by selling government securities, by raising the "discount rate" (interest which the Federal Reserve charges commercial banks for borrowing money), or by raising the amount of "demand deposits" member banks must keep in the nearest Federal Reserve Bank.

**Wholesale Price Index** — This index shows changes in prices of approximately 2,400 commodities such as chemicals, farm products, fuels, leather, lumber, machinery, metals, paper, rubber and textile products which are bought by wholesale businesses. It measures prices against a base of 1967 in the same way that the Consumer Price Index does. The Wholesale Price Index is also known as the Producer Price Index.

**Working Capital** — This is money required to buy the things needed to turn out goods and services, items such as purchases and supplies. Although these things by themselves do not produce wealth, they enable the fixed capital to do so. In accounting terms, working capital refers to the excess of quickly convertible assets over current liabilities. *Fixed capital,* on the other hand, refers to things like airplanes, trucks, machinery, power plants and buildings which are used to create more wealth by producing goods or services.

## PUBLISHERS' ADDRESSES

Addison-Wesley Publishing Co.
1 Jacob Way
Reading, MA 01867

AMACOM
Division of American Management Association
135 West 50th Street
New York, NY 10020

American Arbitration Association
140 West 51st Street
New York, NY 10022

American Management Association
135 West 50th Street
New York, NY 10020

Arco Publishing, Inc.
215 Park Avenue South
New York, NY 10003

Ashton-Tate Books
10150 West Jefferson Boulevard
Culver City, CA 90230

Aurea Publications
P.O. Box 176
Allenhurst, NJ 07711

Ayer Co. Publs., Inc.
P.O. Box 958
Salem, NH 03079

Barron's Educational Series
113 Crossways Park Drive
Woodbury, NY 11797

Betterway Publications, Inc.
Box 81
White Hall, VA 22987

Bill Communications, Inc.
633 Third Avenue
New York, NY 10017

Books on Demand
300 North Zeeb Road
Ann Arbor, MI 48106

Bowker, R.R.
245 West 17th Street
New York, NY 10011

Brookfield Publishing Company
Brookfield, VT 05036

Bureau of National Affairs
Inc., 1231 25th Street, NW
Washington, DC 20037

## PUBLISHERS' ADDRESSES (continued)

Butterworth's, 80 Montvale Avenue
Stoneham, MA 02180

Caddylak Publishing
201 Montrose Road
Westbury, NY 11590

Carrey, D.W.
6256 NW 16 Court
Margate, FL 33063

Charter Oak Press
P.O. Box 7783
Lancaster, PA 17604

Columbia Books, Inc.
1350 New York Avenue, NW
Washington, DC 20005

Columbia University Press
562 West 113th Street
New York, NY 10025

Commerce Clearing House, Inc.
4025 West Peterson Avenue
Chicago, IL 60646

Conference Board, The, Inc.
845 Third Avenue
New York, NY 10022

Contemporary Books, Inc.
180 North Michigan Avenue
Chicago, IL 60601

Cornerstone Press
1230 Avenue of the Americas
New York, NY 10020

Council of State Governments
P.O. Box 11910
Lexington, KY 40578

Dartnell Corp., The
4660 Ravenswood Avenue
Chicago, IL 60640

David and Charles, Inc.
P.O. Box 57
North Pomfret, VT 05053

Directory of Corporate Affiliations
3004 Glenview Road
Wilmette, IL 60091

Dow Jones-Irwin
1818 Ridge Road
Homewood, IL 60430

## PUBLISHERS' ADDRESSES (continued)

Dun & Bradstreet
299 Park Avenue
New York, NY 10170

Executive Enterprises, Inc.
33 West 60 Street
New York, NY 10023

Facts on File
460 Park Avenue South
New York, NY 10016

Fairchild Books & Visuals
7 East 12th Street
New York, NY 10003

Farnsworth Publishing Co., Inc.
78 Randall Avenue
Rockville Center, NY 11570

Franklin, Burt, Publishing
234 East 44 Street
New York, NY 10017

Franklin Watts, Inc.
387 Park Avenue South
New York, NY 10016

Free Press
866 Third Avenue
New York, NY 10022

Freedom Press
P.O. Box 5503
Scottsdale, AZ 85261

Gale Research Co.
Book Tower
Detroit, MI 48226

Dower Publishing Co.
Brookfield, VT 05036

Halsted Press
605 Third Avenue
New York, NY 10158

Harper & Row Pubs., Inc.
10 East 53rd Street
New York, NY 10022

Hempstead House
1019 Jerome Street
Houston, TX 77009

Holt, Rinehart & Winston—No longer in business

Houghton Mifflin Co.
1 Beacon Street
Boston, MA 02108

## PUBLISHERS' ADDRESSES (continued)

IMS Press
426 Pennsylvania Avenue
Fort Washington, PA 19034

Industrial Development Division
Institute of Science and Technology
University of Michigan
2200 Bonesteel Boulevard
Ann Arbor, MI 48105

Inflation Reports
P.O. Box 60148
Los Angeles, CA 90068

Institute for Business Planning, Inc.
B & P Marking
Route 9W
Englewood Cliffs, NJ 07632

International Commercial Service
P.O. Box 4082
Irvine, CA 92716

International Ideas, Inc.
1627 Spruce Street
Philadelphia, PA 19103

International Publications Service
242 Cherry Street, Philadelphia
PA 19106

International Trade Books
401 North Broad Street
Philadelphia, PA 19108

Interstate
19 North Jackson Street
Danville, IL 61832

Intertrade Index Printing Consultant
PO Box 636
Federal Square
Newark, NJ 07101

Iowa State University Press
2121 South State Avenue
Ames, IA 50010

Irwin, Richard D., Inc.
1818 Ridge Road
Homewood, IL 60430

Jane's Publishing, Inc.
115 Fifth Avenue
New York, NY 10003

Johnson Publishing Company
1880 South 57th Court
Boulder, CO 80301

## PUBLISHERS' ADDRESSES (continued)

Jossey-Bass, Inc. Publishing
433 California Street
San Francisco, CA 94104

Lodestar Books
2 Park Avenue
New York, NY 10016

Longwood Publishing Group, Inc.
51 Washington Street
Dover, NH 03820

Machinery and Allied Products Institute
1200 18 Street
Washington, DC 20036

McKay, David, Company—out of business.

Macmillan Publishing Company
866 Third Avenue
New York, NY 10022

McGraw-Hill, Inc.
1221 Avenue of the Americas
New York, NY 10020

Merriam, G & C Company
Merriam-Webster, Inc.
PO Box 281
Springfield, MA 01102

Michigan State University Press
1405 South Harrison Road
East Lansing, MI 48824

Monarch Press
1230 Avenue of the Americas
New York, NY 10020

Moody's Investors Service
99 Church Street
New York, NY 10007

National Association of Accountants
PO Box 433
Montvale, NJ 07645

National Retail Merchants Association
100 West 31 Street
New York, NY 10001

New American Library
1633 Broadway
New York, NY 10019

New York State School of Industrial Relations
Cornell University
PO Box 1000
Ithaca, NY 14851

## PUBLISHERS' ADDRESSES (continued)

New York Times
229 West 43rd Street
New York, NY 10036

Nolo Press
950 Parker Street
Berkeley, CA 94710

Oceana Publications, Inc.
PO Box 156
Na' Alehu, HI 96772

Official Airline Guides, Inc.
2000 Clearwater Drive
Oak Brook, IL 60521

O'Dwyer, J.R.
271 Madison Avenue
New York, NY 10016

Oxbridge Communications, Inc.
150 Fifth Avenue
New York, NY 10011

Oxford University Press
200 Madison Avenue
New York, NY 10016

PacTel Publishing
1600 South Main Street
Walnut Creek, CA 94596

PCW Communications, Inc.
501 Second Street
San Francisco, CA 94107

Peterson's Guides, Incorporated
166 Bunn Drive
Princeton, NJ 08540

Pharos Books
200 Park Avenue
New York, NY 10166

Practicing Law Institute
810 Seventh Avenue
New York, NY 10019

Praeger Publishers
521 Fifth Avenue
New York, NY 10175

Prentice-Hall
Englewood Cliffs, NJ 07632

Preston Publications, Inc.
P.O. Box 48312
Niles, IL 60648

## PUBLISHERS' ADDRESSES (continued)

Princeton Research Institute
P.O. Box 363
Princeton, NJ 08540

Princeton University Press
41 William Street
Princeton, NJ 08540

Public Service Materials Center
111 North Central Avenue
Hartsdale, NY 10530

Ragan, Lawrence, Communications, Inc.
407 South Dearborn
Chicago, IL 60605

Random House, Inc.
201 East 50 Street
New York, NY 10022

Reader's Digest Association
Pleasantville, NY 10570

Reston Publishing Co., Inc.
Prentice-Hall
Englewood, NJ 07632

Revisionist Press
P.O. Box 2009
Brooklyn, NY 11202

Russell's Guides, Inc.
834 Third Avenue SE
Cedar Rapids, IA 52406

St. Martin's Press, Inc.
175 Fifth Avenue
New York, NY 10010

Scott, Foresman & Co.
1900 East Lake Avenue
Glenview, IL 60025

Standard & Poor Corporation
25 Broadway
New York, NY 10004

State Mutual Book and Periodical Service
521 Fifth Avenue
New York, NY 10017

Sunset Books
80 Willow Road
Menlo Park, CA 94025

Superintendent of Documents
U.S. Government Printing Office
Washington, DC 20402

## PUBLISHERS' ADDRESSES (continued)

Thomas Publishing Company
1 Penn Plaza
New York, NY 10001

Times Books
201 East 50th Street
New York, NY 10022

Toll Free Digest Co., Inc.
Claverack, NY 12513

Transatlantic Arts, Inc.
PO Box 6086
Albuquerque, NM 87197

Transportation Guides, Inc.
111 Cherry Street
New Canaan, CT 06840

Unipub
205 East 42 Street
New York, NY 10017

University Press of America, Inc.
4720 Boston Way
Lanham, MD 20706

Van Nostrand Reinhold Co., Inc.
135 West 50th Street
New York, NY 10020

Viking-Penguin
40 West 23 Street
New York, NY 10010

Volunteer, The National Center for Citizen
    Involvement
1111 North 19th Street
Arlington, VA 22209

Wall Street Journal
200 Burnett Road
Chicopee, MA 01020
(for subscriptions only)

Warner Books
666 Fifth Avenue
New York, NY 10103

West Publishing Co.
P.O. Box 4526
St. Paul, MN 55102

Willamette Management Associates, Inc.
400 Southwest Sixth Avenue
Portland, OR 97204

Wilson, H. W.
950 University Avenue
Bronx, NY 10452

## PUBLISHERS' ADDRESSES (continued)

Wolcotts, Inc.
15124 Downey Avenue
Paramount, CA 90723

Writer's Digest Books
9933 Alliance Road
Cincinnati, OH 45242

Ziff Communication Co.
1 Park Avenue
New York, NY 10016

# Index